THE LAMPMAN
SYMPOSIUM

RE-APPRAISALS:
Canadian Writers
Department of English, University of Ottawa
General Editor: Lorraine McMullen

THE
LAMPMAN
SYMPOSIUM

Edited and with
an Introduction by
LORRAINE MCMULLEN

Photo courtesy of the Public Archives of Canada

Copyright 1976 for the authors
by the University of Ottawa Press, 1976

ISBN-0-7766-4383-5

The Lampman Symposium

Edited and with an Introduction
by **LORRAINE MCMULLEN**

University of Ottawa Press
Ottawa, Canada, 1976

487/84

ACKNOWLEDGEMENTS
Grateful acknowledgement is made to the Canada Council for the financial assistance which made the Lampman symposium possible and to the Faculty of Arts, University of Ottawa for providing the funds for publication of this volume.

L.M.

Printed and bound in Canada.

CONTENTS

INTRODUCTION

The third annual symposium on Canadian literary figures held May 2 to 4, 1975, at University of Ottawa differed from those of previous years in focussing on a nineteenth-century writer. Papers dealt with a wide variety of topics of concern to Lampman scholars, from biographical and textual problems to Lampman's place in the context of English literature generally and Canadian literature specifically.

The opening biographical panel provoked immediate debate with Chairman Fred Cogswell's introductory remarks challenging the entire concept of the biographical approach to literature. The first panelist, Margaret Whitridge, insisted strongly on the relevance of the author's personal life to his work and directed her remarks particularly to Lampman's love for Katherine Waddell, an area of his experience thus far relatively unexplored. Dr. Whitridge's paper published here is an elaboration of her informal remarks on this panel. Scholars will welcome the guide to Lampman manuscripts and letters also prepared by Dr. Whitridge for inclusion in this volume. The two following panelists approached the topic from different points of view. Ralph Gustafson recalled the impression he had formed of Lampman from discussions with Arthur Stringer and Duncan Campbell Scott, two writers who had known him personally; Barry Davies voiced his interest in the intellectual biography, an interest his paper the following day was to make even more evident.

In the first address of the morning Michael Gnarowski directed attention to a number of mysteries related to Lampman, reminding the conference that such a focus was in keeping with the two preceding symposia on Grove and Klein. Professor Gnarowski recommended for consideration such unresolved issues as Lampman's relative happiness or unhappiness in Ottawa, the nature of his relationship with Katherine Waddell, the missing Lampman portrait by Edmond Dyonnet, the unknown contents of the Lampman manuscript notebook at Simon Fraser University, and Lampman's relative lack of success as a published writer in spite of the excellent reception accorded his first volume. Not all of these issues were resolved at the conference, of course, although Dr. Whitridge did explore the first two to some extent, and it is anticipated that her forthcoming biography of Lampman will further illuminate these two areas; and Bruce Nesbitt in his address Sunday made reference to some of the contents of the Simon Fraser manuscript notebook.

Over half of Lampman's published poems are sonnets, and thus it is appropriate that three of the symposium papers dealt with this aspect of his art. First was Carl F. Klinck's paper on "The Frogs." Interestingly, Professor Klinck directed attention to the poem most frequently alluded to in subsequent papers and to an issue which was to surface a number of times during the conference: the various interpretations of "dream," a term which recurs insistently throughout the Lampman canon. Discussion of the sonnets continued later with Louis MacKendrick's wide ranging paper in which he presented a detailed study of techniques, diction, imagery, and themes of Lampman's sonnets. Professor John Nause's paper the following day, "The Theory and Practice of Craft," augmented this examination of Lampman's craft. Louis Dudek in his address "Lampman and the Death of the Sonnet" went beyond the Canadian frame of reference to view Lampman's sonnets in the context of the English sonnet and its development from the seventeenth century. Professor Dudek sparked some debate with his assessment of Lampman as a successful yet conservative sonneteer for his time when compared with such practitioners as Gerard Manley Hopkins and William Butler Yeats.. Some conference members felt that more attention should be given to the Canadian context of Lampman's sonnets and that the significance of Charles G.D. Roberts' landscape sonnets should be recognized. In the final paper Saturday Dick Harrison took yet a different approach to the Lampman poetry, contrasting the poetic worlds of Lampman and Duncan Campbell Scott in a study of the sources and means of resolution of pain and fear in their poetry.

The second day of the symposium began with Barrie Davies' examination of some of Lampman's philosophic and aesthetic bases. While Professor Davies referred to both Emerson and Thoreau in his detailed presentation, he interpreted Lampman's philosophic stance as basically Platonic. His paper, then, may be seen as directed to a central issue broached in different ways by Professor Klinck and others, and one to which Professor Sandra Djwa drew attention in the final panel: the relative importance of the Platonic and the Emersonian to Lampman's philosophic outlook.

Bruce Nesbitt's paper the final afternoon proved to be to some extent a development from his address to the 1972 Conference on Editing Canadian texts. He re-asserted the necessity of going back to the Lampman manuscript notebooks to recover the poet's final intentions, and stressed the inadequacy of available evidence — textual, biographical, and cultural — by which to evaluate Lampman's importance to Canadian literature. It was with considerable interest that symposium members questioned Dr. Nesbitt regarding the implications of the manuscript notebook and other papers acquired by Simon Fraser University to the establishment of a definitive Lampman text.

The final panel chaired by Carl F. Klinck explored the nature and scope of Lampman's achievement and returned to some of the problems still to be resolved. The ideas of the panelists were clearly and cogently presented, and happily four of the panel members have made their comments available for publication in this volume. In his remarks, D.G. Jones demonstrated that "Lampman's vision has proved archetypically Canadian," and both Professor Jones and James Steele spoke of Lampman's link with Canadian modernist poets. Robin Mathews reminded us of the importance of Lampman's Canadian milieu, especially the intellectual milieu, to his artistic expression. Sandra Djwa referred to the complex problems involved in editing a definitive edition of Lampman and to the yet unresolved issue of Lampman's philosophic and religious positions.

The most important aspect of this symposium was its effectiveness in providing a forum for debate and assessment of current scholarship and for consideration of the direction which future Lampman studies should take. Left unrecorded in this collection of symposium papers is the vigorous, sometimes heated, discussion which followed the papers and continued into coffee and luncheon breaks and into evening receptions, and the impact of the Saturday evening readings of Lampman poems on all present. It became obvious during the conference that there is still much to be done; for example, biographical and textual studies are as yet incomplete and are essential for more extensive critical analyses; and the cultural and intellectual milieu of the Confederation period requires further exploration. However, Lampman's place as a major literary figure has been clearly confirmed and his centrality to a study of Canadian literature established.

LORRAINE MCMULLEN

RALPH GUSTAFSON

LIFE AND NATURE: SOME RE-APPRAISALS OF ARCHIBALD LAMPMAN

What I shall say will be from memory, judgment and love; not a work of research. I shall, I suppose, be presenting much that has already been concluded. I am not a scholar. I am also not stupid. I believe I can tell a poor poem at the drop of a rhythm. I believe it is important to determine what is a good poem and what is not. In this respect, I welcome a chance to hold forth. I believe that recognizing and propagating good poetry save Canada from sog, sloppiness and selfdelusion.

And so I get into scrapes such as you see me in now. I might as well say it: that I am suspicious of scholarship — that is, unmitigated scholarship. It is too like Procrustes, chopping up or elongating poets to fit his arbitrary measurements, or what is worse, insisting that the poet get in bed with him. I don't like being told that I will never truly appreciate the physical, sensational, sensual, soul-expanding, heartbeating experience of a great line of poetry without knowing whether the line is logaoedic, phanopoeic, or just plain iambic pentameter when it would have been better if the poet had thrown in a trochee. Or worse, that Lampman should have written more socialistic verse.

Another thought struck me when I was assigned to this particular panel on biography: Good God, they think I *knew* Lampman!

Well, I didn't and I do. I have felt near to Lampman on three occasions. I remember when I was living for a time in New York City. I had a letter asking me if I could find a publisher for a long manuscript poem. The request came from Tom MacInnes — that lively, natural, original versifier that never gets grouped with the poets of the Sixties. Subsequently, I met Tom MacInnes' son, Loftus MacInnes, who followed up his father's letter. I find out that the son is married to Lampman's daughter, Natalie. I also felt very near to Lampman when my wife and I were in Ottawa going across the Provinces and up to the Yukon at the expense of that best of all possible friends to poets, the Canada Council. I had my wife take a snapshot of me sitting on the steps of that house, the corner of Bay and Slater Streets, where Lampman lived the last years of his life. We were just in time. The bulldozer was already across the road. I suppose we must not preserve old houses simply because immortality lived in them. Yet, at the time, I was enraged: that demolition was a metaphor of Canada to me — and you know what for. Highrise in the place of inspiration.

Those porch steps I sat on were sad enough — seven leading up to a two-family ordinary three-storey brick dwelling by way of a small Victorian scroll-worked wooden verandah. The prevention of light got me: no windows on the sides except two narrow high-up on the non-neighbour side; one narrow downstairs window and a counterpart above, neither much in conversation with the sun. But I mustn't go on — a poet can write under any circumstances, as Lampman proved — Chaucer in his counting-house, Wordsworth in his cottage, Mandelshtam in his concentration camp. That is my point today — as it was my point in that essay, "Among the Millet," which I wrote long ago for John Sutherland and *The Northern Review* and which Mike Gnarowski has collected in his valuable critical book called *Archibald Lampman*. But that 1959 experience of sadness has persisted — the windows of the house were boarded, the demolition sign was tacked beside the front door. It is as if it were true what the *Canadian Magazine* for February of this year replied to an inquiring reader when he asked: "Could you please tell me about the Canadian poet Archibald Lampman?" The reply is: "A cairn was erected to his memory at his birthplace in Ontario. Yet his personal life could hardly be viewed as either poetic or distinguished." Yes, indeed; that is what the answer is.

The third time that I was drawn very near to the person of Lampman was in 1950. I was invited to read my poems on a programme with Arthur Stringer at the New York Public Library under the auspices of the Poetry Society of America. I had read Stringer's piece, of 1941, called "Wild Poets I've Known" in B.K. Sandwell's *Saturday Night* where verses of both of us sometimes appeared. Arthur Stringer describes Lampman a year before Lampman's death. What impressed Stringer was Lampman's "stubborn inner strength." The judgment is important since so much has been made of Lampman succumbing to fate and environment. I asked Stringer about Lampman and that 1898 meeting at William Henry Drummond's house on Sherbrooke Street in Montreal. What immediately struck him was sensitivity, Stringer told me; "fragile, Lampman looked, but with the strength of a good work of art." Not a bit dreamy-eyed, but with a strong gentleness in his eyes that went with his handshake and the mould of his chin (one can see that chin without "the smallish yellow-brown beard" Stringer says Lampan wore, in the portrait at the front of the 1925 edition, *Lyrics of Earth*). Stringer said that the gentle but nevertheless piercing look of Lampman held a reminiscence of the portrait of Keats (I should think that Stringer had in mind that miniature of Keats by Joseph Severn). I, in turn, was reminded of Lampman's remark that he felt he was a faint reincarnation of Keats. The loveliest phrase of Stringer's is that sentence in his article that Lampman "did not carry the torch it seemed to me; he was the torch itself." In his conversation with me, Stringer was emphasizing that the hallmark of Lampman was not morbidity, but sensitivity combined with inner courage; charm and humour.

"Do not think of me as a hollow-eyed spectre on the verge of dissolution, suffering perpetual pain." This, Lampman said of himself not a year before he died. Lampman may have had the look of fragility, a Shelley-like spirituality, in outward appearance; inwardly he was like Keats who licked the bully who was abusing the kitten. You remember how Lampman flared up at William Wilfred Campbell's vanity.

Duncan Campbell Scott in a letter to me disliked my reference to "poor Johnny Keats" as a reminder to the state modern critics were putting Lampman in, even though I used the phrase only to deplore it. Scott was right. We have had enough of "poor, melancholy Archibald Lampman." We must not turn Lampman into some sort of case-history definable only out of a psychiatric word-book. Since Freud, the biographical tendency has been to turn all poets into case histories out of which they tried to write themselves. On the contrary, I think of Renoir tying his paint-brush to his paralyzed arm. The true poet is not kept from his poem unless fate dastardly slaps him down. Take away his girl, face him with death, — but give him a piece of paper after an adequate meal and see what happens.

Of that spirit is Lampman. "Lampman is not the victim of nefarious Ottawa." I said that long ago. I tested the conviction with Duncan Campbell Scott. He warned me against over-emphasis on Ottawa; against overplaying the restriction of Lampman's environment. "Lampman never wanted to be a man of affairs or felt sense at failure to be such," Scott wrote me. "The cast of Lampman's nature was not toward melancholy." I agreed. The word "melancholy" is to be disliked; it smacks of an induced mood; an indecision of mind; of masochism. Lampman uses the word about himself. But not in those pliant and indulgent senses. When Lampman uses the word he is saying a disguised other; he is saying, "I want to write a great poem"; he is saying that life is sad. Lampman suffered what all poets suffer — indeed, what all sensitivities suffer — an awareness of the inadequacy of things, an awareness of a sadness that grows and descends overwhelmingly the further behind we leave ignorance — a world theme that occupied Lampman long before he got to Ottawa. *Lacrimae rerum*. The discords of existence, the bitter awareness that is so desperate in our own day with its exaltation of violence and its sacrifice of innocence. The

3

awareness is no less valid for Lampman. He uses a stronger word than 'melancholy.' "I am becoming morbid, subject to dreadful moods and hypochondria." Lampman does not mean what we mean by 'hypochondriasis': a condition of morbid anxiety about the health, in which a diseased organ is thought to be present... Lampman had none of this, Just the opposite. He did not know,he did not believe he was doomed until the end. Lampman's mind was healthy. It is more likely that Lampman's exclamations were induced by the fact that his wife was harassed by her servant than that the world was not socialistic.

I am not being trivial. Sorrows enough as reasons, Lampman had: his father in agony from cancer; the death of a son; a troubled marriage; his passion for Katherine Waddell. But his own analysis of himself as "morbid" shows how healthy he was. Let Lampman answer us. Our analysis must not rest on phrases wrenched out of context. "I am constitutionally sensitive to a morbid degree," he writes, but the letter goes on to tell us that the morbidity sprang from his inability to push his way among men. "I am a great coward when it comes to taking hold of practical affairs." He was embedded in drudgery, but, says Lampman, "not very heavy drudgery." (July 5, 1893). "My position is very comfortable and... any change would probably be for the worse." (October 26, 1894). Lampman in his essay, "Happiness: A Preachment," defines happiness as "the consciousness of adequate self-expression." Here is the good solid ground if you want the key to Lampman's condition. Out of the knowledge of a good poem well-written, he had "Magnificent enjoyment!" he exclaims (July 5, 1893). He is dejected because of his inability at self-criticism of his poetry. "I am becoming morbid," he says, and in the same letter he exclaims, "There is one thing about me that may be safely said. I am certainly not stagnating: on the contrary, I become more sensitive, more excitable, more nervously alive with every year." (February 28, 1894). And so the phrases go. I am not minimizing. I am clarifying. And best of all, the most fetchingly loveable moment in all these letters I quote from, is that moment (July 5, 1897) when Lampman writes his friend Thomson, editor of the *Youth's Companion* in Boston, "I wish," Lampman wishes, "I could sell something to your confounded paper — I want to buy a bicycle." In that same year he wanted to paint "the town crimson."

Let us cashier this portrait of a morbid poet bedraggled by routine; this portrait of a despondent socialist. John Sutherland in his criticism of Lampman makes the conflict between dream — a word so frequent in Lampman's poetry — and "reality" — the word which Sutherland wants Lampman to come to — he makes the conflict a sign of morbidity and goes on to say that, anyway. Lampman was imitating Poe and Matthew Arnold. Let me point out that what you imitate, you aren't. Louis Dudek in his criticism follows pretty much the stricture of Sutherland. Let me define the word "dream" as used by Lampman: it meant, not unreality, not vacuity; dream meant living, it meant meditation. In 1883 Lampman wrote his college friend, J. A. Ritchie: "I have grown wonderfully prolific of verse since I came here [to Ottawa]... I have long evenings to myself and invariably fall adreaming, which always ends in the shooting of a new subject across my brain." So, when you read in the poem "Snow":

I
As secret as yon buried stream,
Plod dumbly on, and dream,

don't think that it is cud-like. For Lampman, to "Dream" is to feel "the essence of the scene in which he finds himself" — as E.K. Brown puts it in his Introduction to *At the Long Sault:*

Dreams are real,

Lampman tells us in "The Frogs." When Lampman uses the phrase "nor think but only dream," he is sharing that apostrophe of Keats when he exclaims in his letter to Benjamin Bailey. "O for a life of sensations rather than of thoughts!" Both poets were simply saying that truth cannot be known by "consequitive reasoning."

As for trying to push Lampman into social poetry so that we can admire him, that is barking up the wrong tree. Lampman was not cut out to be a socialist poet; he was a nature poet. We social sophisticates may not like that phrase "kinship with nature" and feel that it is ducking out of responsibility into a never-never land. But deprive Lampman of this and you deprive him of what he spoke of in writing about Emerson: "Elemental joy... the eternal movement of life." Shall we have a prose declaration by Lampman on the subject? Here it is: "I do not care a hang for anything but poetry."

We are told that Lampman's social poems are the better poems. This is wrong. It is evidence of a critical fallacy. The fallacy is a left-over from F.R. Leavis' critical position when, in assessing the accomplishment of T.S. Eliot, he sets up the decay of civilization as the measure of literary insight. The fallacy identifies literary merit with social vision. Dudek is guilty of this in his essay "The Significance of Lampman" and, unfortunately, Margaret Whitridge pursues the fallacy.

Looking sharply at the political facts of life is a predominant attitude in Canadian poetry. Before Lampman's time, there is the amazing Miss Crawford. This girl scathingly denounces General Wolseley's treatment of the Zulus under Cetewayo ("War"). Contemporary with Lampman, there is that neglected poet who could well be, in part, the subject of one of these symposia, George Frederick Cameron, who with passion attacks tyranny in Cuba, who regards poetry as "sacred rage." Political alignment with freedom is one of the hallmarks of Canadian poetry from the time of Alexander McLachlan. So, too, are the headlines of the day apotheosized by Milton, Wordsworth, Yeats, Auden. But not because of their social awareness do their poems last; it is because they are good poetry.

Of Lampman, his friend Edward William Thomson was right: Lampman ought to have discharged his political philosophy in prose; it would have kept it out of his verse. For in truth, the least good of Lampman's poems are those with explicit social content. Current critism is exalting all the wrong poems; "To a Millionaire" is exalted over "A Winter Evening." Dudek wants Laurentian black flies and the whining mosquito in Lampman's winter evening. At that moment, they were out of season. This critical stance is inverted romanticism. All black flies are good: peaches aren't.

Where Lampman is most moralistically social, he is poorest in his poetry. His poems about usurers, poets, politicians and ultra-protestants are exercises; they read like something out of a manual. You can't experience the poem, you can only think it. We are told; not shown. We are given unspecific rhetoric. The verse is expository. The diction, chill. We lack the immediate experience. We want "the curly horns of ribbed icicles"; not the text that leaves the moral. There is only one thing equally insupportable: the diction of those nature poems overblown with late Victorian poetics. They read like Palgrave's Treasury with pressed roses in it. One wishes, on both scores, that Lampman had taken more walks in the winter night, had sat in the summer heat the more. Try as I do, I cannot regard "The City of the End of Things" other than a pastiche, a grade B movie; unmoving and cliché.

Duncan Campbell Scott conjectured that Lampman at the end of his life tended "towards the drama of life and away from the picture of nature." I think not. Or not exactly if by drama of life we mean an extraversion into the inequities of social structures. I agree if by "drama of life" is meant more human emotion; Lampman's drama of life was not historical but immediate and personal. I think he would have given over such excursions into drama as "At the Long Sault" where the drama is synthetic. With all possible deference to Margaret Whitridge and her Introduction to the reprinted volumes of poetry by Lampman, "At the Long Sault" is not "mature mastery" and "The culmination of [Lampman's] poetic development." That poem isn't. Nor did Lampman influence the "social and literary advances made in twentieth century Canada." Lampman has had little influence. The influences have been outside Canada: Yeats, Eliot, Pound through William Carlos Williams.

Lampman wanted to get out of cities and circumventing reminders and routine, not into social politics. He took refuge where all intelligence can find refuge, in things natural. The act of doing so is not as escape, it is a correction. Lampman was quite aware that without throwing himself under the wheels of the juggernaut, he could engage his life on behalf of life. The joy did work unconditionally and often.

I strayed through the midst of the city
Like one distracted or mad.
'Oh, Life! Oh, Life!' I kept saying,
And the very word seemed sad.

I passed through the gates of the city,
     And I heard the small birds sing,
I laid me down in the meadows
     Afar from the bell-ringing...

Blue, blue was the heaven above me,
     And the earth green at my feet;
'Oh, Life! Oh, Life! I kept saying,
     And the very word seemed sweet.

Exhibit A.

THE SOCIAL POEMS OF LAMPMAN
     The question to be asked is this: Would Lampman's art have developed better under urban conditions? (Connor p. 119)

The social poems Dudek mentions as better:

DESPONDENCY (p. 107 in Whitridge): *entirely abstract (what Pound cut out of Yeats); not a sharp image in it except the first line.*

THE POETS (p. 113) *All statement — though I rather like his thought of poets "with their goatish smell."*

THE TRUTH (p. 114) *All statement; the admonition is to be still even if you burn with the truth.*

KNOWLEDGE (p. 110) *You can't experience the poem: you can only think it. But N.B. "to think and dream."*

AN OLD LESSON (p. 111) *Carman's sermon. We all should become a lily.*

VOICES OF EARTH (p. 218): *A list; lists are no good in poems, despite Homer.*

TO A MILLIONAIRE (p. 276) *All the sonnet lacks are a purple light and a hiss or two.*

THE MODERN POLITICIAN: (p. 277) *Unspecific rhetoric.*

TO AN ULTRA-PROTESTANT (p. 285) *And just think: this is next door to "A January Morning," p. 286, and still the former is preferred!*

AVARICE (p. 285) *Avaunt!*

Exhibit B

NOTES — LAMPMAN
I rather think that ending to L's poem "Heat" echoes Dante Gabriel Rossetti's "close-companioned inarticulate hour" in No.XX, "Silent Noon". There is no sensual embrace in Lampman, but let him have his "inarticulate hour" just the same.

L is not "A follower of dreams with nothing in his hands" as Carman is in his poem "Sweetheart of the Sea."

A poem is not to be praised because of its subject matter.

The brevity of life pitches Lampman into sadness, not "The City of the End of Things."

L's "deep pessimism" justifies his refuge in nature.

Dudek says "the keynote of L's poetry is the resistence of his self-honesty to the pull of his idealism". One cannot make a cheat of Lampman.

One cannot be morbid with a sense of humour. L found reading Homer in the original Greek "a good deal easier" than reading Browning.

L berates the stoic as austere and hostile to joy: "Stoicism is not happiness; it is armed peace." (see L's essay "Happiness")

Revelatory rather than achieved = most contemporary Canadian verse.

One grave flaw in L's make-up: he did not like Brahms.

L bears with me: poetry is a moral procedure. His final and chief criterion of poetry always comes back to "Does this man contribute to the welfare of humanity?"

When L says "True art must be naive", he is not akin to Carman, he is referring to the "wonder" that Keats supplies.

"Nothing except his fellow creatures," L said, "can ever bore a man who has learned the satisfaction of contemplating a tree."

L lived in age when the Toronto "Globe" could ask: "Should we have Sunday street-cars?"

L finds beauty in frogs. Pound found beauty in a tin of sardines (see his poem "The Study in Aesthetics").

MARGARET COULBY WHITRIDGE

LOVE AND HATE
IN LAMPMAN'S POETRY

Archibald Lampman's poetry, like his personality, was infinitely more complex than is commonly realized, a fact which was pointed out by Desmond Pacey in *Ten Canadian Poets*.[1] Pacey also accurately located the source of Lampman's late-developing pessimism as a "combination of personal misfortune and the apprehensive temper of the age in which he lived," as well as situating it in time: "It was in the eighteen-nineties that Lampman's personal distress became acute."

While recognizing the tension that exists in the poet's work, a number of critics have failed to pinpoint the exact cause of the nightmare that took possession of Lampman when he was thirty. Ironically, long and rather tedious narrative poems like "The Organist", "Ingvi and Alf", "The Monk" and "The Little Handmaiden" have been cited as examples of the poet's rare venturings into emotional depths. Consequently Lampman's "Love lyrics" have been hastily dismissed as so inept as to be considered little more than inexplicable lapses of taste.

The time is now due to consider the poet's personal life from a new and different perspective which has greater potential of illuminating the important latter half of his literary life. Lampman was undoubtedly not just a nature poet obsessed with the necessity of creating an aesthetically satisfying, perfect stanza or completing the cycle of the seasons in the symbolic, abstract image of a circle. His well developed social conscience led him early into the paths of socialism. His *love* — as well as his love of art and music and classical civilizations — inspired him to write, during his brief lifetime, at least one hundred and seventy sonnets. Each one is built concisely and carefully upon one consequential

9

idea into the remarkable beauty and unity of a single, complete expression. Each reveals exactly what the poet was thinking and feeling on a particular day in his life. Each is a photograph of the poet's mind, set against the physical background of Ottawa's landscape, the Gatineau Hills or the lakes and forests of Quebec.

Two fundamental factors were among the guiding forces which tempered the poet's life and became important subjects of his writing — love and, most significantly, rejection.

The newly published volume, *Lampman's Kate — Late Love Poems of Archibald Lampman*,[2] will, it is hoped, strengthen the realization of the importance of the love-hate relationship in Lampman's writing, as in his life. Perhaps it will add a new element of understanding to use in estimating and evaluating the precarious balance of opposites and the restless tension so evident in Lampman's later work.

Lampman as a man was both sensitive and sensuous. His nature was impulsive, passionate, generous and affectionate. He was a romantic, immediately receptive to women and, from the time he was seventeen years of age, he was always deeply in love. The object changed and the sentiment deepened, as did his capacity for pain, with the passing of time, but the objective remained always the same.

In September 1879, as a freshman at Trinity College in Toronto, the teen-aged boy was caught up in the social and creative opportunities which had suddenly opened to him. His previous horizon had been no wider than the Anglican rectory in Cobourg and Trinity College School, a private, Anglican, boy's preparatory school in Port Hope, Ontario. In Toronto, Lampman enjoyed the excellent company of his cheerful, congenial classmates. He also immediately liked several attractive and intelligent young women to whom he was introduced. He found them remarkably emancipated compared to the background of late Victorian life he had known in the United Empire Loyalist settlements of eastern Ontario.

These enchanting young women, about whom Lampman began writing poems outlining their charms and his sentiments, were the sisters of his college friends or the daughters of his professors. They were members of well-off professional families or they were politically aware due to the influence of famous fathers. And, they were accustomed to the theatre, art galleries, musical concerts and the latest in books and fashions. Lampman liked them because they were sensitive, well-educated, poised and had been exposed to the same ideas to which he was so responsive. Several girls had travelled abroad and could talk knowingly of life in New York, London and Paris.

At eighteen, Lampman was a slim, dark, young man, a bright and witty student interested in everything and well-liked by his fellow students. He was thoroughly enjoying his newly found freedom and widening perspectives in Toronto. At first meeting, he appeared a quiet, rather shy person with a serious expression and a pleasing manner. He was fastidious about his personal appearance and while his clothes were inexpensive tweeds and his shoes cheap, his shirts were white and starched, his ties carefully chosen and the total effect one of pride. The poet's brown hair curled above his ears, his eyes were brown and expressive, his chin firm. The hint of a moustache outlined his upper lip. He sang lustily and rather well, smoked a pipe, enjoyed a beer with his friends and customarily stayed up very late at night. Lampman was a good student and had the capacity to be a brilliant one except that he was easily distracted, especially by the current "Rosamund" in his life.

In the spring of 1882, when he was barely twenty, Lampman's thoughts were undoubtedly turning to other things than his studies. His new involvement may help to explain his slipping marks and his undistinguished final standing in his graduating class at Trinity College that year. The range of his poetic expression was certainly expanding and he was trying secretly to express an important facet of his nature in the poems he was producing.

An unpublished poem written in March 1882 can be found among his manuscripts in the collection of the Public Archives of Canada in Ottawa.[3] Untitled — and, indeed, no title is necessary — it defines his interest:

> Ah, strangely sweet are thy great grave eyes
> And their passionate blue is bright,
> Like the changing hues of the strong sea waves
> That darken and fade in the light.
>
> And who can fathom those sweet blue eyes
> Or the thoughts that dwell in thee,
> That ebb and flow like the mighty floods
> In the great, deep heart of the sea?

It was the first of many love poems written by the poet, although he offered only a few, written to his wife during their courtship, for publication. Another unpublished fragment written about the same time gains from its informal style, from the blank verse in which it was written, and from the natural diction which catches the poet's mood late on a winter night, alone with a girl:

> Oh, have you not often loved to stand and forget and surrender?
> For see, there is nothing but snow and the white river around us,
> No sound but the stir of the wind in the grey of the whispering snowdrifts,
> And nothing above but the night and the stars in the infinite silence... [4]

While he was attending university in Toronto, Lampman formed an enduring friendship with May Blackstock, a handsome, spirited, intelligent young woman, who later became a professional musician. They understood each other extremely well and later corresponded until the end of Lampman's life but it is unlikely that these early love poems were written to her because May was several years older than the poet and she was already engaged to be married to a young man named McKeggie.

A few months later, in the summer of 1882, Lampman graduated from Trinity College. He spent a few weeks near St. Catharines, with his uncle and aunt to whom he was very devoted, and then moved into a bare hotel room in Orangeville, Ontario and started teaching school. After four miserable months, he returned briefly to Toronto for Christmas and moved to Ottawa in January 1883 to take up his appointment as a clerk in the Post Office Department of the federal civil service. He was soon in love again, this time with a young woman named Charlotte to whom he began writing charming love lyrics like "Ballade of a Love-Fancy", dated October 4, 1883. At the same time, the thread of melancholy which is woven through most of his adult life was finding expression in poems like "Despondency" and the very interesting, unpublished poem, "Carnaval of the Leaves," also written in October 1883. The poem concludes on an almost frantic note:

> All frenzied mortals who have life and breath
> Clasp hands, join lips and take their fill of glee;
> The grave fulfils and faster whirls the throng;
> Redder the wine runs through the desperate days.
> The dance growns louder, wilder grows the song,
> The kisses sharper, as the blue plague slays;
> So the leaves fall and death is wide to smite.
> Haste wind, make revel for a day and night.[5]

A year later, in October 1884, Lampman began writing his first sonnets to Maud Playter, the fifteen-year old daughter of a prominent physician, whom he had recently met and by whom he was totally enamoured. The series of a dozen sonnets, which spanned the three years of their courtship, was published partly by Lampman in *Among the Millet* in 1888. The total sequence was published by E.K. Brown and D.C. Scott in *At the Long Sault and Other New Poems by Archibald Lampman* in 1943. These sonnets were too stylized and idealistic to have ready emotional credibility but their interest was assured by the beauty created by the poet out of his emotional involvement.

Unfortunately, passion is not necessarily a sound basis for a permanent relationship like marriage and, within three months, Lampman was penning poems like the sonnet, "The Faithful Lover",[6] to reassure himself that:

> Even as the faithful lover who may see
> Some flowers of women lovelier than his own,

he still would cling, "With stronger love and sweeter faith to her". A few scant months later, he was writing poems like "Silence!"[7] counselling

> Thou fool, be still, for thou canst never guess,
> By thy loose words, so base and pitiless,
> How many hearts, how many times, are stung.

Sometime in 1889, about eighteen months after his long-awaited marriage to Maud, Lampman feel deeply in love with a fellow clerk in the Post Office, Miss Katherine Waddell of Ottawa. For a man who was so advanced in his thinking, Lampman's dilemma was typically and tragically Victorian. He wanted to divorce his fragile and dependent young wife of nineteen in order to marry a forthright and emancipated woman of thirty. It was, simply, impossible.

One can imagine the criticism he endured even from those who knew and liked him best. Duncan Campbell Scott, who had been best man at Lampman's wedding, resolutely refused to think about the matter. His chief at the Post Office, William LeSueur, himself a writer of note, offered friendly counsel and tried to cool the affair, while encouraging the poet to develop his literary career. Lampman's wife stormed and retreated into physical illness and nervous collapse. Katherine Waddell's widowed mother objected. The eminent Dr. Playter and his wife, who had strongly disapproved of their young daughter's marriage to a penniless clerk, were appalled and their family life was seriously disturbed. At first, they encouraged the couple to try and resolve their differences and they offered financial help and a home under their roof to Maud and Lampman, and his family. Finally, the Playters uprooted and returned to Toronto to live.

Maud's only sister, Kate, was permanently affected by her sister's unhappiness. She grew bitter and felt unable to marry. Later it was she who assumed the major responsibility of raising the·Lampman children, Natalie and Archie.

Lampman himself had mixed emotions during the last ten years of his life. He did not hate Maud, nor could he blame her. He felt sorry for her situation and was agonized over his own. From time to time, they attempted, fairly successfully, to seal the breach and it appears that on each occasion, a child was born to them. In 1894, they shared profound grief when their first son died, probably of typhoid fever, when he was about six months old.

Eventually, after five or six frustrating years which must have been alternately exciting and depressing for both Lampman and his lady, Katherine Waddell made it clear that any permanent kind of relationship was impossible and their intimacy, whatever its nature had been, was finished. They continued to see each other at work; Lampman continued to love her from afar; they remained friends. Until the week before he died, he continued to write poems to her in his rough manuscript notebooks — poems it is unlikely she ever saw. Apart from the six sonnets published as "Portrait in Six Sonnets" by Scott and E. K. Brown in *At the Long Sault and Other New Poems by Archibald Lampman*, it appears that most of the love poems to Katherine Waddell were written between 1894 and 1897 when, presumably, their romance had flowered and was in the process of blowing. During 1894 and 1895 the poems alternate between passionate attraction and a real intimacy, distraught recognition and cold terror, when he realized that she was permanently lost to him.

Early in 1895, Lampman wrote of Katherine Waddell, in a verse fragment:

> She....
> Makes all my blood and all my spirit stir
> Whose lips are sweeter than my thoughts of her
> Whose little bosom is more soft to me
> Than any other even in my dreams could be
> Whose touch is but the warm awakening....[8]

Yet, in October of that year he was bitterly penning:

> Couldst thou buy know my secret heart,
> The sorrow that I dare not tell,
> The passion that with bitterest art
> I hide so well — ....
>
> Ah, couldst thou know this and descry
> The sorrow and the dull despair,
> Wouldst thou but smile and pass me by
> Or wouldst thou care?[9]

On October 15th, he acknowledged:

> You cannot answer to my love.
> I know it and I ask it not.

But, nonetheless,

> Yet, haply, you might spare a while,
> When nearness urges to forget,
> Some special tenderness of smiles
> To me, your friend, without regret.[10]

Six months later, Lampman was still dreaming about his love and acting out his desires:

> And I, touched by a sudden, sweet surprise,
> Caught you in both mine arms with sobs and sighs
> And kissed your brow, beloved, and your lips.

while she returned his sentiment:

> And you — ah yes! even you, upon my breast
> Leaned for a moment, with cheeks wet and wan,
> Then smiled and vanished....[11]

14

No doubt the poems derived from actual experience, thinly veiled in deference to the Victorian morality from which they could not escape. Probably in response to a rebuke he asked,

> How then could I be near you — hark and see —
> And not be touched, not love you utterly?[12]

A year later, on August 5, 1897 Lampman, in a poetic allegory of forty-eight lines, now given the title "A Summer Figure", described his beloved, asking nature, whom he customarily personified to".... touch her eyes/Till they widen, deep and grey" as she stands,

> Dreaming at the break of day,
> Pure and silent, rapt and far,
> Like the spirit of a star.

He watches and notes:

> See her dreamy countenance,
> Ah how quickly, melt and change
> And her laughter flash like light
> Out of darkness, deep and bright....
>
> Touch her with some deeper thing,
> Something human and naive;
> You shall see the sorrow spring
> To her closing lips and leave
> Traces in her earnest eyes
> Of old wistful memories....
>
> Mark ye, how the branches bend
> Round her softly parted hair,
> How the sunshine crowns my friend,
> Tall and slender, straight and fair.
> Hardly shall another be
> Beautiful and bright as she.[13]

It is obvious that even at that date Lampman still loved his lady and that she was still responsive to "old wistful memories". Yet only a few months from that time, late in 1897, Lampman made the last step to resignation; he and his wife were reunited physically and mentally and their last child, Archibald Otto was born a few months later. In a poem, which was not the final one Lampman wrote about his love, but did mark the final step in their relationship, he accepted her decision:

> Only the dream of you I keep,
> The dream that must be always by,
> The memories that will not sleep,
> The griefs that make me want to die.
> So far apart, at last, are we!
> Once you could smile; you smile no more,
> Closed are the blinds and locked the door,
> Such is the bitterness of Fate to me![14]

Lampman's last poem written to Katherine Waddell was the sonnet beginning "You talk of age, my friend, to whom life's prime," (Number 4, in the sequence, "Portrait in Six Sonnets" written on January 29, 1899 the week before he died). In the sonnet, he who knew he was dying, sought to reassure her that the best of life was not already past. It was a subject which bothered her and they had discussed it before; as early as 1896 he had written a longer poem to tease her out of her fear of old age, "Old Indeed Are you", but evidently he had not succeeded. His own predicament was then so serious, his physical strenght almost completely exhausted, that it is a wonder that he could yet be concerned for her welfare.

He and his wife had earlier made their peace. A few months before, in the sonnet, "Uplifting" he had described their compromise:

> We passed heart-weary from the troubled house
> Where much of care and much of strife had been,
> A jar of tongues upon a petty scene;
> And now as from a long and tortured drouse,
> The dark returned us to our purer vows:.....[15]

Lampman had, just before their marriage, truly foreseen the end result of their union in "A Forecast":

> What days await this woman, whose strange feet
> Breathe spells, whose presence makes men dream like wine,
> Tall, free and slender as the forest pine,
> Whose form is moulded music, through whose sweet
> Frank eyes I feel the very heart's least beat,
> Keen, passionate, full of dreams and fire:
> How in the end, and to what man's desire
> Shall all this yield, whose lips shall these lips meet?
> One thing I know: if he be great and pure,
> This love, this fire, this beauty shall endure:
> Triumph and hope shall lead him by the palm:
> But if not this, some differing thing he be,
> That dream shall break in terror; he shall see
> The whirlwind ripen, where he sowed the calm.[16]

Lampman sowed alienation and he had been forced to endure the whirlwind of his discontent. Out of it he wove a poetry that defied the Victorians. It is impossible to forget or to separate the love/hate theme in his work.

NOTES
[1] Desmond PACEY, *Ten Canadian Poets* (Toronto, Ryerson, 1958), pp. 114-140.

[2] Margaret WHITRIDGE, (editor). *Lampman's Kate — Late Love Poems of Archibald Lampman* (Ottawa, Borealis, 1975) pp. 1-52.

[3] *Lampman Papers*, Volume 2 (Ottawa, Public Archives of Canada).

[4] *Ibid.*

[5] *Miscellaneous Lampman Manuscripts*, Library of Parliament (now retained in Public Archives of Canada) p. 18

[6] *Lampman's Kate, op. cit.*, p. 26.

[7] *Ibid.*, p. 27.

[8] *Ibid.*, p. 38.

[9] *Ibid.*, p. 37.

[10] *Ibid.*, p. 36.

[11] *Ibid.*, p. 41.

[12] *Ibid.*, p. 45.

[13] *Ibid.*, pp. 48-49.

[14] *Ibid.*, p. 52.

[15] D.C. SCOTT (editor), *The Poems of Archibald Lampman* (Toronto, Morang, 1900) p. 290.

[16] *Ibid.*, p. 117.

MICHAEL GNAROWSKI

ARCHIBALD LAMPMAN
AND HIS CRITICS

The title of this paper is "Archibald Lampan and his Critics," an all-embracing notion which, however elastic one's conscience, one is promoted, nevertheless, to define more narrowly and specifically. What better way, then, to go about the strict business of specifics, than by going off on a tangent which, hopefully, after some zigging and zagging, should bring us back to the real concerns of the paper.

Puttering about with Lampman and Lampman materials, I have been struck by the number of 'mysteries' — if mysteries is an overly dramatic term — then we could call them 'problems' which appear to invest the work and circumstances of this writer. For examplen there is the problem of Lampman's happiness/unhappiness with the city — Ottawa — in which he lived, and his position in the Federal Civil Service. There is the problem of Lampman's friendships, with, as a further instance, his visits to the painter Edmond Dyonnet who lived in Montreal, and who is supposed to have entertained Lampman and his cronies on several occasions in his bachelor digs, and to have drawn or painted a Lampman likeness the mysterious disappearance of which Professor Munro Beattie laments in his admirable essay on the poet.[1] The mystery here is partly that of the portrait, but, more interestingly, a diligent search through the unpublished typescript of Dyonnet's autobiography has revealed not a word about Lampman. There is, as well, the mystery of all the unpublished poetry tucked away in a literary nest-egg and unconscionably delayed in its hatching these last several years. Or, there is the mystery if all those tid-bits excised — both in fact and in fiction — by party or parties unknown from some of Lampman's extant letters; or the mystery of Lampman's relationship with Katherine Waddell, a

19

delicate situation now being probed — some would insist, obsessively — by researchers. Well, not to be outdone, one proposes a mystery of one's own, a mystery which is offered to the faithful who gather at symposia. This mystery which is less mystery and more a simple problem, has to do with Lampman's critical reception and its bearing, such as it may be, upon his history as a published writer.

In an introductory essay to a collection of critical materials dealing with Lampman, written six years ago, I dwelt on the fact that Lampman's mature career spanned a period of eleven years and included three collections of verse, in all of which he had a full hand, although he did not live to see *Alcyone* in its final, published state. I should have added that two of the three collections — *Among the Millet* (1888), and *Alcyone* (1899) were published privately by Lampman, and that he experienced considerable difficulty in placing his middle volume with a publisher until Copeland and Day, again with some problems, brought a very modest, fifty-six page book, *Lyrics of Earth* (1895?)[2] Generally speaking, both literary historians and critics have not attached particular significance to the fact that (i) Lampman apparently had to rely on his own resources and not those of an established publisher to ensure book publication for something like eighty-five per cent of his verse, and, (ii) that his critical reception appears to have had no impact in persuading prospective publishers to secure Lampman's work for their lists. The problem, which offers itself more as a double-barrelled question, .is worth considering.

In attempting any kind of an answer to the questions implicit in Lampman's published history, it might prove to be useful to compare his situation with the situations of those of his contemporaries with whom he is most frequently lumped under that totally unsatisfactory label: the Confederation Poets. Taking that span of time — 1888 to 1899 — which must be seen as the Lampman period, we note that while there is no neat falling into place on the part of the four poets whose careers are thus being studied comparatively, there is, however, enough substantial overlap in the middle ground to make a comparison interesting and, perhaps, significant.

In the first instance, every one of Lampman, Carman, Campbell and Scott, arranged for the private publication of his first collection of verse. Roberts, whose *Orion...* came out under the Lippincott imprint in Philadelphia is the exception. Secondly, while Lampman produced three collections between 1888 and 1899 for a rough total of three hundred and seventeen pages of poetry, W.W. Campbell had four books in the same period; and Carman, eight for almost the same span of time, two of which were smallish 'Vagabondia' books which he co-authored with Richard Hovey. For the years 1886 to 1898, Roberts had four titles plus *Orion...*; and D.C. Scott, usually seen as a late-comer to the movement, published two books of poetry and a collection of short stories in the years 1893 to 1898. But the real import of this 'head' count of individual volumes is not that it illustrates a much more measured and moderate approach to publication on Lampman's part, but that it brings us face to face with the question with which we introduced this contribution to the canon of Lampman mysteries. Why, for example, was Lampman unable or unwilling to try for a wider audience which established commercial publication might have secured for him. This, incidentally, is not a question applied to some reclusive poet, but it is asked of the career of an individual who was chronically dissatisfied with his lot, and anxious to augment a civil service salary about which he complained on more than one occasion. This, also, having to do with a poet who was patently conscious of a large reading public to which he addressed himself through the pages of periodicals such as *Harper's, The Atlantic Monthly, Scribner's* to name the most prestigious — and they were prestigious, cultural magazines of their time with a wide and respectable circulation, There were many others: *Century, Current Literature, Independent, Canadian Magazine, The Chap Book, Youth's Companion, The Week*, and so on. The solution to Lampman's problem, then, seems, to us, to have lain in a successful approach to an established publisher capable of insuring a good sale, and, consequently, a decent royalty. One raises this point because all the other poets of Lampman's group quickly found reputable publishers to undertake their work. In the period which we are considering, W.W. Campbell secured Briggs (Ryerson) of Toronto, and Houghton, Mifflin of Boston and New York as his publishers; Carman alternated between Copeland and Day, Lamson Wolffe, and Small Maynard of Boston; and Roberts, after an initial appearance under the Lippincott imprint, placed his books with Briggs and Copp Clark of Toronto, and Lothrop, and Lamson Wolffe of Boston. Duncan Campbell Scott published with Copeland and Day during the period in question.

The upshot of all this is that there were half a dozen publishers who proved to be accessible to this group of poets, and many of these were Boston publishers to whom few if any one Canadian poet would or could come as highly recommended as was Lampman — and this by no less a figure than that mandarin of literary life, William Dean Howells. To compound the problem further, and to squelch the notion that it may very well not be the critic's or historian's business to probe the reasons for Lampman's having published only three books in his life, we know that there survives at least one draft collection of sonnets which Lampman had hoped to see into print (unsuccessfully), and it is as a writer of sonnets that Lampman had been praised most generously and strongly by the critics and reviewers of his time.

This, then, bring us to another part of the Lampman question, and is has to do with the nature of Lampman's reputation with those critics who were his contemporaries. Carl Y. Connor in his biographical study — a work originally undertaken as a doctoral dissertation, and which, to this day, forty-six years later, still stands as the only full scale appraisal of the poet, develops a valuable discussion of the circumstances and the critical reception of both *Among the Millet* ans *Lyrics of Earth*. Of Lampman's first collection, he says:

With the publication of *Among the Millet* in 1888, Lampman at once took a definite and rather high place in the ranks of Canadian writers.[3]

He then goes on to cite and to quote from some of the more prominent reviews of the time. The review of Agnes Maule Machar who used the *nom de plume* of Fidelis, and who wrote in the March 22, 1889 issue of *The Week* is a study in praise and reservations. Ms. Machar had a strong and wilful mind of her own, and Connor quotes, with a kind of disapproving wonder, her slighting of the poem "The Frogs"; her reservations about the title poem "Among the Millet," and her implied advice to Lampman to stay away from "longer descriptiveness" which, Ms. Machar felt had "a certain unsatisfactoriness." But there was strong praise in that review as well. From an opening assertion that this collection proves that there is a Canadian Literature:

> The people who are always asserting that we have no literature and no poets to speak of must take some trouble to avoid looking into volumes like that recently given to us by Mr. A. Lampman.[4]

to the statement that this volume:

> ... represents *real work*, as well as imaginative power, delicacy of perception and vivid faithfulness of description, as well as a high degree of general artistic excellence and careful *technique*.[5]

to the concluding remark that:

> ... [these poems] are not of the class that can be dismissed in a word as 'meritorious verse', but are worthy of the careful appreciative study ...[6]

In short, and in spite of its reservations, the review was a strong endorsement for Lampman's first book. Among other reviews, there were two items in the *Trinity University Review*, a periodical published by Lampman's College. The first was a reprint (less quoted material) of a review which had appeared in the *London Spectator*. The anonymous "transatlantic relative" as the critic was described, had a generous measure of praise for the Ottawa poet. He opened by saying:

> A volume of verse published at Ottawa, and full at once of the influence of Canadian scenery and of classical culture, arrests the reader's attention at once. And though there is nothing exactly demonstrating true genius in this volume, there is so much in it of truth, simplicity, vivacity, and of something that fairly deserves the name of passion, that it is very pleasant and sometimes even impressive reading, almost from beginning to end.[7]

But then, having dwelt on the charm and graphic realism of some of Lampman's sonnets, the London critic took issue, for almost half of the review, with what he/she described as Lampman's attitude to the "modern spirit." What worried this individual was the poet's professed attitude which "delights to sit holding no form of creed, but contemplating all," and, moreover, that Lampman wrote of truth "as if loyalty to it could only be adequately proved by silence and the refusal to limit it by any sort of enunciation."[8] There was more troubling matter. The sonnet in which Lampman describes the poet as "half-god, half-brute," and also as "half-brutish, half-divine, but all of earth," was diagnosed by the critic as follows:

> There is in that sonnet the same tendency to exaggerate the force of the lowest element in the imaginative life which belongs to the pessimism of the day.[9]

But then, all could be well again:

> Perhaps, however, Mr. Lampman is at his best in his fine pictures of the Canadian scenery.[10]

And, in conclusion:

> Mr. Lampman can write verses in which there is a true 'lyrical cry'.[11]

The *Trinity University* Review was clearly determined to give extended notice to the work of an alumnus of the College, and some months after running the piece from the *London Spectator*, Graeme Mercer Adam[12] produced his own appraisal in the December 1889 issue of the magazine under the heading "Two Recent Volumes of Canadian Verse." The books under review were W.W. Campbell's *Lake Lyrics and Other Poems*, and Lampman's first collection. Adam permitted himself an ironic aside which poked sober fun at the proliferation of native bards, and he quoted, in mock seriousness from Lighthall's *Songs of the Great Dominion* to the effect that:

> ... the number of Canadian writers who have produced really good verse [as having been] set down as three hundred.[13]

Of *Among the Millet*, Adam began by saying:

> If anything good ever came out of Ottawa it is this volume of Mr. Lampman's.[14]

He then went on:

> He [Lampman] is at once a scholar and artist. ... He has imagination, insight, and sustained powers of reflection ... much of his verse is the outcome of his classical training, and in this respect the poet is not likely ever to be popular.[15]

and, later:

> ... like Roberts, also, he seems rather to repress than obtrude his nativism, though here and there in the volume the national characterictics reveal themselves.[16]

The review then focussed on "Among the Timothy," "Between the Rapids," and "Winter Hues Recalled" as being good examples of poems which gave particular evidence of "their Canadian origin." The poems, said Adam:

... speak no less of the poet's sympathy with Nature, though the manifestation of that sympathy is always under restraint. More than in any other of our poets does philosophy enter into his work. In this respect Mr. Lampman reflects the spirit of the age even while he is most lyrical. In a large portion of his verse the contemplative vein appears, the sonnets most of all being enriched by a deep thoughtfulness.[17]

So much from Graeme Mercer Adam; agreeing in part but also expressing a firmly polite variance in opinion from the reviewer of the *London Spectator*. This, in turn, carries us to the notice which William Dean Howells gave *Among the Millet* in his column "Editor's Study." Writing in the April 17, 1889 issue of *Harper's New Monthly Magazine*, Howells quoted the sonnet "Truth," parts of "The Frogs," and the poem "Heat," and, besides being full of a kind of general and generous praise of Lampman, he made the claim of having discovered the Canadian poet. He said:

> ... a poet on our list toward whom we feel something of the high and sacred self-satisfaction of discovered ....[18]

Later, American critics would go one better and look upon Lampman as an American poet.[19] All in all, it is probably fair to say that even a modest sampling of reviews such as this, shows that *Among the Millet* was well received. In addition, and while it is true that Lampman was some time between his first and second books, his name and reputation were served by articles and notices which appeared in various journals and periodicals of the time. This, as well, being complemented by the appearance of individual poems which he continued to publish at a steady and impressive rate in the foremost magazines of his day. There were other forms of editorial patronage. For example, *Trinity University Review* ran a pointed notice of one paragraph in its April 1890 issue. This echoed an earlier call in Graeme Mercer Adam's review for government patronage on behalf of Lampman. It reads in part:

> We are glad to see that some of the more influential of the Canadian newspapers have recently been urging upon the Government the claims of Mr. Lampman for promotion in the Civil Service, in which, at present he occupies a position not as lucrative nor as congenial as it certainly ought to be. That Mr. Lampman's distinguished position amongst Canadian men of letters should be thus recognized by the Government none can dispute ....[20]

The following year, in the Wednesday, August 12, 1891 issue of the *Boston Evening Transcript* there appeared an extended notice of Lampman's projected visit to that city. While, as the *Transcript* reported:

> New York is now suffering from a mosquito wave, and the whole town is agog with excitement and irritated cuticle in consequence ....

Boston

> ... is to have a visit shortly from a poet who is already attaining a high distinction in the world of letters ....

So enchanted is the columnist — who signed himself "The Listener" — by the prospect of the visit, that he welcomed Lampman with a smothering and possessive embrace:

> Mr. Archibald Lampman is a Canadian, but the Listener regards it as a great mistake to speak of him as 'a Canadian poet'. Such a phrase is much too limiting. If a man is really a 'Canadian poet' — if he has expressed Canada in his verse — he is also an American poet. A man might be an American poet without also being an English poet, but he could not be a Canadian poet without also being an American poet. It is not merely that he speaks the same language; he breathes the same air; plucks the same flowers, hears the songs of the same birds, rests beneath the same trees under the same scorching summer sun .... Moreover, the social conditions about him, which always affect a real poet profoundly, are pratically the same in Canada as in the United States, in spite of all humbugging talk about monarchical institutions on the one side and republican institutions on the other.

More interestingly, perhaps, this columnist, in addition to mentioning such well-known Lampman poems as "Truth," "In October," and "The Frogs," and after quoting from "Freedom," said:

> Mr. Lampman is certainly original and distinctly modern; though he does not follow the most modern methods of versification. No one but a thorough modern could have written that short poem "Heat" ....

Generally, then, the Listener came across as a friendly and appreciative supporter of Lampman. There would be other articles and notices: A.W. Crawford's piece in the December 1895 issue of *Acta Victoriana*, subsequently reprinted in the Critical Views Volume on Lampman (1970), as well as Joseph Dana Miller's evaluation of Lampman, Carman, Roberts and Campbell in an article entitled "The Singers of Canada" in the May 1895 issue of *Munsey's Magazine*. Miller proves to be a remarkably wide-ranging and perceptive writer. He begins with a speculation on Canada's destiny and identity with the following statement:

> Whether it be the ultimate destiny of Canada to be merged with the United States or to continue as a separate nationality, or dependency, is a political problem which may have an important bearing upon the Canadian literature of the future. But in either event her intellectual individuality is not likely to perish.[21]

He then goes on to show — in a general fashion — a strong and intelligent sense of the make-up of Canadian culture. Folk-lore, the two languages, the religious spirit, are all taken into account, and Miller then allows himself an important observation:

> ... when we turn to the group of younger poets whose work is the most notable feature of contemporary Canadian Literature, we are immediately struck by a predominant strain of originality, of natural freedom ... The singers are not mere echoes. Their strong unfettered verse comes of no transplanted origin; it is full of native vigor, of individual strength and charm.[22]

Miller's article is really a composite of several capsule pieces on the more prominent Canadian poets of the generation, and, for example it includes comment on Pauline Johnson and Frederick George Scott. On Lampman, Miller gives a thumbnail biographical paragraph together with the following critical estimate:

> Mr. Howells ranks Lampman with the strongest of American singers. His knowledge of nature is something more than intellectual — it is affinitive ... the grass, the sky are not merely furnishings of Lampman's verse, but the utterance of a close and genuine sympathy. And these objects, as he sees them, are transfused by a fancy never rising, perhaps, to the full strength of imagination, but soft, delicate, dreamy ....[23]

In 1895, Lampman published — with the help and influence of E.W. Thomson — his second, smallish collection of poems — *Lyrics of Earth*. A review note in *The Dial* for September 1, 1896, says that Lampman "sings of nature because he knows her, not because he takes it to be the literary fashion," and concludes its extended paragraph with:

> Mr. Lampman's verse combines this fidelity to the facts of nature with high qualities of imagination and passion,...[24]

The Critic for January 16, 1897, in its compressed review echoes what is becoming, in Lampman's case, a refrain:

> Mr. Lampman is a keen observer and strong lover of Nature ... His work is refined and clear, rich with imagery and melodious ... There is a freshness, a simplicity, a naturalness about Mr. Lampman's work which gives to it a distinction nowadays quite unusual.[25]

In March of 1897, *Current Literature* gave Lampman the benefit of a review article which featured six of his poems. Following the usual bit of biographical introduction, the reviewer then added:

> While there are others in the field, Mr. Lampman comes the nearest to being Canada's poet of nature, although nearly all Canadian poetry is marked by an absence of the restless and unhealthy spirit which mars so much contemporary verse.[26]

and went on to paraphrase what Joseph Dana Miller had written two years earlier in *Munsey's Magazine*.

At this point in Lampman's history, one begins to sense a kind of falling off of critical enthusiasm. All seem agreed that Lampman is a fine and true poet. But the slim, fifty-six page *Lyrics of Earth*, sure and fine as the verse may be, appeared to be too slight to overpower the critics. There were, as well, voices of disaffection which were raised from time to time. Gordon Waldron is an example. In an article subtitled "A Criticism" which appeared in the December 1896 issue of *The Canadian Magazine*, Waldron took aim at Campbell, Carman, Roberts and Lampman. He was surprisingly tough:

> The poets, [he says] having won the ear of a generous and patriotic, though un-

critical press, have been raised to an imposing authority, which restrains all originality and all determined devotion to poetry as a fine art.

It is therefore, important that these writers should be critically examined. If they be found to be not true poets, but blind leaders of the blind, they should be deposed, and the hope of a distinctively Canadian literature may be one step nearer its realization than it now seems to be.[27]

But then, heretical dissenters like Waldron were particularly rare in the last years of the nineteenth century, and it is Ernestine Whiteside who was nearer to the critical consensus when she wrote in *The McMaster University Monthly* in November 1898:

Lampman excels in his sonnets. The perfection of finish and gem-like brilliancy necessary to the sonnet is his characteristic. For dramatic effects he is not qualified ....

... The ruling characteristic through all Lampman's poetry is his passion for beauty. His descriptions are so fine, sympathetic and true, yet so infused with an artistic idealization ....[28]

Lampman's life, however, was drawing to a close, and the spate of substantial criticism a record of which fills much of two and a half pages of entries in Watters and Bell, *On Canadian Literature, 1806-1960*, would appear after the posthumous publication of the collected edition of the Poems.

There is a curiously touching and entirely genuine tribute to Lampman written by a friend and correspondent — albeit somewhat distant — William D. Lighthall. In his own, fugitive periodical called *The Horizon*, Lighthall published in the first number, dated January 1903, Lampman's "The Land of Pallas" preceded by these remarks:

With all our jabber about the practical, and our running after millions, and this or that mark of place and position, have we not to admit in the secret deposit vault of our hearts, that it is the missionary, the working slummer, the idealist who does something, who, after all, are the real 'noblesse' the real great, the real successful and even the real rich. They are certainly the real happy ... If Canadian Universities paid the attention they should to such men, he [Lampman] would have been with us yet ....

That it was not so is another proof that these institutions are largely out of touch with the living movements around them. Lampman keenly felt the need of new national ideals in our country.[29]

It may well be that our own time is beginning to feel, keenly, the need for a closer examination of Lampman's performance as poet and thinker; it may well be, as well, that we could stand less orthodoxy in our critical conclusions.

NOTES
[1] "Munro Beattie on Archibald Lampman," in *Our Living Tradition* [:] *Seven Canadians*, First Series, C.T. BISSELL, ed., 73.

[2] Some insight into this process is provided in Peter E. GREIG'S article "A Check List of Lampman Manuscript Material in the Douglas Library Archives," in *Douglas Library Notes* XVI:1:12-27 (Autumn 1967).

Confusion regarding the date of publication of *Lyrics of Earth* stems from the fact that while the title page bears the date 1895 in Roman numerals, there is a notation to the effect that the book was published in March 1896. Lampman's correspondence, some of which is reproduced in Mr. Greig's article points to 1896 as the true publication date.

³ Carl Y. CONNOR, *Archibald Lampman, Canadian Poet of Nature* (New York/Montreal, 1929), 96.

⁴ [Agnes Maule MACHAR], "Some Recent Canadian Poems," *The Week*, VI, March 22, 1889, 251.

⁵ *Ibid.*

⁶ *Ibid.*, 252.

⁷ ANON., "A Canadian Poet," *Trinity University Review*, 11, March 1889, 37.

⁸ *Ibid.*, 38.

⁹ *Ibid.*

¹⁰ *Ibid.*

¹¹ *Ibid.*

¹² Graeme Mercer ADAM (1839-1912) publisher, writer and literary journalist, remembered for his editorship of *The Canadian Monthly and National Review*, his brief association with John Lovell of Montreal, and his sharing of the views of Goldwin Smith for whom he managed the *Bystander*.

¹³ G. Mercer ADAM, "Two Recent Volumes of Canadian Verse," *Trinity University Review*, II December 1889, 153.

¹⁴ *Ibid.*

¹⁵ *Ibid.*

¹⁶ *Ibid.*

¹⁷ *Ibid.* 154.

¹⁸ [William Dean HOWELLS], "Editor's Study," *Harper's New Monthly Magazine*, LXXVIII, April 1889, 821.

¹⁹ See "American Poets of To-day: Archibald Lampman," *Current Literature*, March 1897, 246-247.

²⁰ "Mr. Archibald Lampman" under "Editorial Topics," in *Trinity University Review*, III, April 1890, [I].

²¹ Joseph Dana MILLER, "The Singers of Canada," *Munsey's Magazine*, XVIII, May 1895, 128.

²² *Ibid.*, 129.

²³ *Ibid.*, 130.

²⁴ *The Dial*, XXI, September 1896, 124.

²⁵ *The Critic*, January 16, 1897, 39-40.

²⁶ ANON., "American Poets of To-day: Archibald Lampman," *Current Literature*, March 1897, 246.

²⁷ Gordon WALDRON, "Canadian Poetry: A Criticism," *The Canadian Magazine*, VIII, December 1896, 101.

²⁸ [Ernestine WHITESIDE], "Canadian Poetry and Poets II," *The McMaster University Monthly*, VIII, November 1898, 68-69.

²⁹ [W.D. LIGHTHALL], "Archibald Lampman's Canada," *The Horizon*, [No.I], January 1903, 7.

CARL F. KLINCK

"THE FROGS": AN EXERCISE IN READING LAMPMAN

Several generations of students have attempted to persuade me that Archibald Lampman was an "escapist" — a temperamental post-office clerk whose "mooning" in the fields around Ottawa was a rather queer rejection of the ways of "life" of more realistic and useful people in that town. The implication that he neglected domestic, social and civic activities has also been alleged by some critics. "The Frogs," a poem published in 1888, has been thought to be a quite damaging expression of such escapism.

The purpose of this article, therefore, is to propose a different reading of "The Frogs." The positive meaning of the poem will be stressed, for, if Lampman could escape *from* something, should there not be a closer examination of what he escaped *to*?

He needs no lame excuses. Even frog-listening betrays no cloudy thinker and no lazy "nature-boy." From the latter charge he has long ago been cleared by Duncan Campbell Scott in the introduction to *Lyrics of Earth* (1925)[1] and by Professor Munro Beattie in *Our Living Tradition* (1957)[2] These writers have fully substantiated the picture of Lampman as Ottawa knew him apart from his writings, and as common-sense must now see him: a normally-industrious civil service employee, a Fabian socialist, a pipe-smoker, a family man, a good companion, and a witty talker. His devotion to "external nature," in the sense of flowers, birds, seasons, landscapes, and solitary places will not be disputed; he enjoyed the physical exercise, the sensations of walking in the open air, the release from strain — as hundreds of pedestrians did in this pre-auto-mobile age. What distinguished him was his keen and articulate response to his natural environment.

29

But thereby hangs the argument. To what extent, and, in what way, was he articulate? Did he make himself understood? on can find agreement that he was a master of sensuous detail, of description of natural scenes, of re-created moods, and, as Duncan Campbell Scott said, of sympathetic "vibration" with nature.[3] Many readers and critics have been content to minimize the substance of Lampman's thought and theory and to consider him a belated disciple of a probably-misunderstood Keats in the late nineteenth-century period of decadent estheticism.

A poem like "The Frogs" has, no doubt, contributed to an uneasy feeling of pleasure and confusion in such readers. The word "dream" occurs nine times in one form or another with apparently a variety of meanings. The *frogs* are "dreamers"; *Earth* has her "spirit's inmost dream"; *Earth* dreams...musing on life; the *air* stands "in a dream" (identified as "reverie"); the eyes of the *frogs*...dream "beyond the night and day"; the dawn finds *them* "unaltered in [their] dream"; *we* are bound "in some divine sweet wonder-dream astray"; and, finally, *we* are "content to dream with you [the frogs]...that...dreams are real, and life is only sweet."

Even Duncan Campbell Scott, a close friend and a respected interpreter of Lampman's poetry, admitted that the latter was characteristically "full of touches that end in the sufficiencies of dreaming and of the loss of personal identity in thought, but when we ask what dreams, what thought, he cannot answer." In many poems, of course, it was evident to Scott and to any other reader that "the substance of [Lampman's] vision" was expressed.[4] But what of "The Frogs"? Does this poem "translate the feeling for nature and life," again the words are Scott's, "into correspondencies in the mind by devices of imagery, of verbal beauty and of cadence."[5] Here, one may give credit to Scott for mentioning, if not explaining, the clues which lead from Keats to Emerson: "feeling," "nature and life," and especially "correspondencies in the mind," these are "transcendentalist" terms and ideas. "Correspondence" is a typical Emersonian touch.

In the famous early essay on "Nature" the New Englander had written:

> Every natural fact is a symbol of some spiritual fact. Every appearance in nature corresponds to some state of the mind, and that state of mind can only be described by presenting that natural appearance as its picture.

Without going into all the premises of this doctrine, or into the philosophical difficulties in proving it, one may, nevertheless, discover in the correspondences of nature and mind — not only on a universal scale, but also in particular aspects — a working hypothesis about Lampman's purpose and the meaning of "The Frogs." In this example of his practice as a nature poet, recognition of Emersonian idealism promises to serve as an explanation and reconciliation of all the various use of "dream."

A certain measure of acquaintance with New England "transcendentalism" may be assumed for Lampman, as well as for Roberts, Campbell, and Scott, particularly because all of them were sons of clergymen and inheritors of religious and idealist thought. If they, and Carman, did not remain manifestly orthodox in religion, they still professed the high moral and spiritual values of Christianity. Nor would the genteel literary climate of the periodicals for which they wrote have been favourable to radicalism or skepticism. These Canadians sold dozens of poems to the most conservative American and Canadian magazines. It must be said, in spite of Lampman's complaints about the parochial restrictions of Ottawa life, that Canadian poets never had, before or later, the extensive public, international recognition, and financial rewards which this Confederation group enjoyed in the 1890s. Realism and naturalism were just around the corner of the century, but editors were still eager to publish little gems of idealistic verse. Touches of vagabondia or bohemianism were the main piquancies which they allowed.

This climate for literature produced several results. One of these was technical, affecting the degree to which ideas needed either full articulation or only suggestion. The response to high thinking, to domestic virtue, or to natural scenery was predictable. These poets could issue the call to spiritual elevation without arguing or delineating meanings; the response they expected was *within* the hearers; they only needed to tease it out. Such rapport enabled them to curtail or avoid sermonizing; mutual understanding allowed the poem to exist, in a rather modern fashion, as a joint product of author and reader. The poem did not need to be an objective statement of *thought*; external detail allowed inward experience to be shaped, assimilated, and shared by the receiving mind of the reader. The method was metaphorical; the whole poem was a catalyst.

This method solved some of the problems resulting from the inadequacy of language in relating matter and mind. Language is a human invention depending upon common agreement about the meaning of certain sounds and signs; so transcendent thought has to be expressed, paradoxically, in words that are earth-bound in origin and in definition. The words "soul," "spirit" and "mind" are commonly regarded as exceptions, for they have been elevated by biblical connotations; yet they are subject to the vagaries of shifting theories. In Emerson these are inclusive terms for all that is "Me" and is thus distinguished from the "not-Me" (or Nature): Christian morality, which survived the loss of Christian orthodoxy, was upheld by "soul" or "spirit" in the context of a personal "self" or intuitive guide. Our word for a related theory might be "mind" as distinguished from the supremacy of reason — some power functioning directly within us by intuitive wisdom and insight beyond the organization of reason. The principal means of communication with this power — or with the biblical "soul" — is the use of metaphor, the suggestive and unique language of the poet.

Reliance upon intuitive self-knowledge can be demonstrated in the works of each of the Confederation poets. Carman in "Vestigia" was not content with the "vestiges" or traces of God seen as footprints, voices, breezes, or gorgeous sunset robes in the natural world; he found that

> God dwelt within [his] heart.

Roberts aspired beyond the "kinship" of nature to know what men only can know,

> the wisdom and the stillness
> Where thy consummations are.

Campbell wrote of

> a greatness that about us lies;
> Within one touch — pervading air and sod —
> That bounds our beings — hidden from our eyes —
> But inward, subtle — linking life to God.

And Duncan Campbell Scott felt on "the height of land,"

> a spell
> Golden and inappellable
> That gives the inarticulate part
> Of our strange being one moment of release
> That seems more native than the touch of time...

Transcendentalism may seem too specifically an American term for such ideas; not only Emerson in New England, but also Wordsworth, Coleridge and Carlyle in Britain had been literary exponents of what was basically an epistemological theory — an emphasis upon intuitive ways of knowing, as checks upon, and correctives to, behaviouristic and rational ways of learning. The influence of the British writers upon Lampman is, of course, not ruled out; it appears to have entered into the many uses of the word "dream" in the nature poems of the Confederation group. Lampman and his contemporaries among the Canadian poets would, no doubt, have preferred the term "transcendentalism" to "supernaturalism," if the latter term implied strong divisions between nature and the realm of mind (spirit). They had no desire to forget the current implications of evolutionary theory. They had quickly come to terms with such ideas and had incorporated Mother Earth and her creatures into a distinctive myth of kinship.

The essential point is that they were not victims of a cultural lag; they were quite aware that their age demanded fresh metaphors to link both the natural and the spiritual in themselves (their selves) and in the universe, metaphors which were neither strictly religious nor the cliches of reasoned-out systems of ideas. They wished, so to speak, to suggest both sides of the coin at once — the side which can be seen and the other which one cannot see but one knows is there. Description was put into the service of wordless self-experience.

There can be no doubt about Lampman's acquaintance with Emerson's ideas. On April 22nd, 1893, "At the Mermaid Inn," a column in the Toronto *Globe*, contained an article written by Lampman which began,

> I do not know whether very many people outside of New England read Emerson's poems, but, if they do not, they ought to.

The conclusion of the article is most significant because it has a bearing upon Lampman's own view of poetry of nature:

> Emerson's sympathy with nature is not, however, in the main that of the observer, the student, or the artist; it is a sympathy of force, a cosmic sympathy. He is drawn to nature because in the energies of his own soul he is aware of a kinship to the forces of nature, and feels with an elemental joy as if it were a part of himself the eternal movement of life.

The voice of Emerson the poet, Lampman asserts, "is like the voice of the pine" in the New Englander's "Woodnotes;" and the pine sings, to the open air, of universal things,

> The rushing metamorphosis
> Dissolving all that fixture is,
> Melts things that be to things that seem
> And solid nature to a dream.

These lines, emphasizing the *melting* of things that be ["solid nature"] to "things that seem" ["dream"], serve rather well as a commentary on "The Frogs," where earth voices are melted into a poet's dream, or, as Emerson wrote in another poem, "Spring still makes spring in the mind." The dream is always the poet's, *in his mind.*.

Lampman did not make the foolish mistake of imputing spirit or mind to frogs, as if he thought that frogs had a green warty side and a hidden cerebral side capable of human intention or human dream. The word "dream" suggests *correspondences*, but not as if universal nature's "dreams" voiced by frogs were the *equivalent in human value* of human dreams. Part III of the poem states that the frogs are dreaming "beyond the night and day," *beyond* what they even dream of knowing. They are voicing sounds which are to them only sounds, albeit perhaps alluring to their mates.

The correspondences of nature and men's minds are cor-respondences grasped by the poet, not by the frogs; that grasp is spon-taneous and direct, defying word-comparisons and idea-connectives. The frog-sounds pass for music of Earth *when the poet hears them* ("And slowly as *we* heard you"), for he has the musical mind which the frogs lack; hence his own word "dream" (not a frog word!) for the meaning of the creatures' mindless singing and for his own wisdom.

Yet the poet's sense of kinship, of belonging to nature, when expressed in metaphor of correspondence, is almost certain to open him to Ruskin's charge of violating logic and committing the alleged sin of "the pathetic fallacy." Indeed, in moments of Spring, the Canadian poet of the late nineteenth century, having assimilated evolutionary notions, could even indulge in the fancy (a meaning of "dream") or the "vision" (another meaning) that the Earth has spoken, without human words, of a harmony even beyond the music of speech — the harmony of man with the whole universe — an epiphany, a view of essential reality, in spite of its evanescence.

There is no surrender in this to either gross naturalism or to exquisite estheticism, to the intellectual emptiness of the non-human or, on the other hand, to the moral emptiness of mere worship of Beauty. One of Lampman's sonnets begins

> Only the things of Beauty shall endure

yet it goes on to refer to Beauty as an "unsought cure" of man, but a "cure" indeed if rightly sought:

> For how can he whom Beauty hath made sure,
> Be proud, or pitiless, play the tyrant's part,
> Be false, or envious, greedy or impure.
> Nay! she will gift him with a golden key
> To unlock every virtue.
>
> . . . .

Beauty makes values "sure." These values, one understands, are not fixed or systematized as if they could be named once-and-for-all, and engraved on tables of stone. Readers who desire an ethic less individual, less fluid, less optimistic about innate goodness, may deplore the lack of formulation in poems like Lampman's. Their attention should be drawn to the true aim of the poet, not to dictate *what* to think, but instead to show *how* to achieve deep, intuitive thinking.

In an apparently naive, but actually sophisticated, way the poet directs and controls the reader's attention through natural scenes until the reader's wisdom supplies the lack of explicit statement. If this is an escape from a linear way of thinking, it is an escape *to* an individual way of response, to felt knowledge rather than "learned" information. Clichés are avoided or re-vivified in the poet's artful selection of "vestiges," traces, connotations, juxtapositions, correspondences, and metaphors — sense — language which is nearest to soul-suggestion. So the reader is not left without guidance as he moves from sense to feeling: from insight and intuition to the highest, but most inexpressible, values — to what he would like to live by.

Characteristically and ideally, such poems of nature by Lampman are total metaphors. They are linguistic constructs paralleling nature's harmonies in the process of conditioning the mind for supersensuous moods of insight, "dreams" of trancendent wisdom, especially hints of superior order. Wallace Stevens described the purpose of such language and such construction in "The Idea of Order at Key West,"

> Words of the fragrant portals, dimly-starred
> And of ourselves and of our origins
> In ghostlier demarcations, keener sounds.

The "educated imagination" of the reader learns to play the game proposed for him by Lampman, whether the poet flatly says, as in "Heat,"

> My thoughts grow keen and clear,

or whether he refrains from tacking on the ending, as in the sonnets "Evening," "A January Morning," and "Winter Uplands". On the other hand, in "The City of the End of Things" and the sonnet "Reality," there is such human violence that no line is necessary to denote an absence of "dream."

As we turn to "The Frogs" it may seem that we have been offered too great a weight of significance for the little creatures to bear. It is perfectly obvious that no other poem of Lampman's contains more uses of "dream." Underline each occurrence of the word and one will find that word running the gamut from a vision in sleep to an ineffable experience such as has been described. The suspicion may be aroused that the rather difficult series of five sonnets entitled "The Frogs" is an ironic exercise in discrimination between the various meanings of "dream" as well as a serious study of the correspondences between nature's being and man's experiences.

"The Frogs" contradicts the notion, so facilely attributed to Lampman, that nature is man's teacher by a simple application of sense impressions. The most inane reading of "The Frogs," therefore, conceives of the little creatures as articulate messengers of Mother Earth's thoughts conveyed to man. One cannot state too often that earth and frogs are not capable of such human language; the apprehension of inward meaning and the use of metaphor are *the poet's* contribution and *the reader's* opportunity. The frogs' voices are to nature what Lampman as a singer is to non-nature, i.e. to the human spirit.

So the true reading must be something like this. The frogs do not speak wisdom; they *breathe* of it. Like Carman's "vestigia," they yield symbolic traces, not statements, to the questing heart. The frogs are "quaint" (unlike us human beings); "uncouth" (not possessed of human consciousness); "flutists" (making sounds, but not expressing human meaning); "murmurers" and "pipers" (not articulate speakers); in short, not communicators with human intelligence.

It can only *"seem"* that, in such auspicious times, the earth may transcend sense and make contact with man's soul and spirit; but it is nothing but a pleasant fancy to hope that frogs can perform the impossible. Earth, in Sonnet II, and the frogs in Sonnets III and IV, are wrapped in *earth's own* dream — that is, in nature's maturity of mating and motherhood. Sonnet V is fanciful again; in the mood induced sensuously by the frogs, the poet indulges in a notion which he knows is not true, but which would please him if it were true, that is,

> That change and pain are shadows faint and fleet,
> And dreams are real, and life is only sweet.

It is well, in understanding Lampman, to observe that the frogs did not enter into conversation with him about the "voices of mankind, the outer roar." It was *the poet* who brought this knowledge of the city with him; it was *he* who contrasted this roar with the pastoral fluting; it was *he* who chose to believe, for the moment, that life was only sweet; it was *he* who felt the sadness of conscious delusion.

It is a characteristic attitude of Lampman to be above such fantasies: he does not clutch at straws. Nor is it true that he typically yields to the mood of the external world. Consider his passion for scenes of winter's icy winds and snow. He presents the external mood, indeed, but he can take it or leave it, yield to it or transcend it. Several of his best-known poems reveal these attitudes. In "Sapphics" there is a reflection of his hard-won spiritual balance or at least stoicism:

> Yet will I keep my spirit
> Clear and valiant, brother to these my noble
> Elms and maples, utterly grave and fearless
> Grandly ungrieving.

The source of his strength is within himself; the elms and maples mirror himself, not he the elms and maples.

The poem which begins

> With loitering step and quiet eye
> Beneath the low November sky

shows that his control is internal. A little "thin light" is not enough to swing the balance of his emotions:

> something in my blood awoke
> A nameless and unnatural cheer
> A pleasure secret and austere.

His cheer is not nature's; his cheer is, in fact, *un*natural — not nature's, not from the outside, but rather from within.

The major criticisms of Lampman's poems thus slide off into ir-

36

relevance. These were not the works of a mere esthete, echoing the echoes of Keats' alleged love-affair with Beauty alone; Lampman aimed consciously at Truth felt in the heart, too deep for words. His poems were not what Wilfred Campbell described as "nature alone ad nauseam."[6] Lampman was not one of the poets who turned "for [their] sole solace and inspiration to the lesson of the pee-wit and the June grass, acquired by the pensive habit of mooning in a present-day Canadian meadow-field."[7]

Lampman provided what Campbell himself demanded, "Nature as the background of the human drama," and, through "correspondences," went beyond background to a profound study of "kinship." His "thees" and "thous" are not Puritan or Quaker in origin; they are intimate words, inviting personal surrender to inspiration. His poems rise, like Wordsworth's skylark, from a nest upon the dewy ground and soar into the rarer privacy of spiritual light,

> True to the Kindred points of Heaven and Home.

NOTES

[1] Toronto: Musson, 1925.

[2] "Archibald Lampman, " *Our Living Tradition*, First Series, edited by Claude T. BISSELL (Toronto: University of Toronto Press, 1957) pp. 63-88.

[3] *Lyrics of Earth*, p. 36.

[4] *Ibid.*, p. 36.

[5] *Ibid.*, p. 32.

[6] *The Evening Journal* (Ottawa), Dec. 3,1904.

[7] *Ibid.*, Sept. 3, 1904.

[8] My article on "The Frogs" was completed before Dr. Sandra Djwa of Simon Fraser University very kindly allowed me to see a copy of her Selected Lampman Concordance and her unpublished manuscript entitled "Lampman's Fleeting Vision." Dr. Djwa had based her comprehensive study upon her unique and accurate index of Lampman's poetic vocabulary; my article had evolved from concentration upon "The Frogs." These different approaches, undertaken independently, have led to divergent interpretations. Dr. Djwa's evidence supports the view that Lampman's uses of "dream" resemble those to be found in Keats, Wordsworth, and Arnold. My own study of "The Frogs" brought me to the conclusion that Lampman's "dream" is closely related, perhaps more closely related, to the concepts of nature, the self, and the poet expressed by Emerson.   C.F.K.

LOUIS DUDEK

LAMPMAN AND THE DEATH OF THE SONNET

You may be wondering about my title, "Lampman and the Death of the Sonnet," whether it is justifiable. Indeed, I ask myself, as I begin this paper, how I can dare to bring up "The Death of the Sonnet" when the sonnets of Lampman, so comforting to read, so good as poetry, are what make him *permanent*. We may think often of the death of Lampman as we read his sonnets; but why "the death of the sonnet"?

Lampman holds so firmly to the truth! He is always honestly himself. Always a strong moralist, a descriptive realist, a sad visionary of nature. And there is nothing clichéd about his nature descriptions and his moral statements. They are all realities, and personal convictions — experiences as he knew them. We get to *know something* as we read sonnet after sonnet. We are not bored with stereotypes. We get to know Lampman.

And yet, apart from the poet himself and the personal interest we find in his poetry, there is always the context in which his work appears. One of the questions that interests us is the question of where literature is going, where Canadian literature is going, and where literature in general, of which the Canadian is a part, is going as a total development. (If you say it is going nowhere, then this is a crossroads where we must argue it out. There is nothing in the world that is not changing, in its own large and coherent ways; and the understanding of this change — at least attempting to understand it — is very much our purpose.)

The context of where literature is going, the oceanic current, takes in Canada and the world. Since we've become interested in Canadian

39

literature, as a national development, we tend to look, naturally, for interrelationships and contexts *within* the literature. And that's very fine. But our study of the internal development of Canadian literature must take for granted, at least — if it does not make it explicit — the relation of this internal history to the larger movements of literature.

The understanding of modernism in Canada — the place of W.W.E. Ross, Knister, F.R. Scott, A.J.M. Smith, Klein, to the Canadian scene and to each other — assumes a preliminary knowledge of modernism and its history outside of Canada. In the same way, Lampman has to be seen in the context of the history of the English sonnet. Taking him only in the Canadian frame of reference might easily lead to mistaken identity and mis-evaluation. And it is therefore in the context of literature in general that we want to see Lampman's performance in the sonnet.

But first I want to introduce a general theory about the development of literature — in fact, about *development* in any system, human or biological, historical or social — a view that I have found useful in my own thinking over many years. It deals with something I call *hypertrophy*. I concocted this word one day out of the Greek roots, to mean "overgrowth," that is, growth that kills, or development that leads to a state of unviability. I pronounced the word *hyperTROphy*. (There was a good pun in the "trophy" — too much success). But the word already exists in medicine, with a different meaning — morbid enlargement of a part or an organ — which is not what I meant, or at least not in that sense of special "growth"; and in medicine it is pronounced *hyPERtrophy*, so that I suppose we must follow the established pronunciation. Anyhow, *hypertrophy*, or *hypertrophic development*.

Anything that is made of constituent parts or elements, and that undergoes development, will tend to arrange these parts in new combinations and relations; it will diminish or add to the existing elements, or it will introduce completely new materials, in order to grow. This growth, in its healthy form, is toward negative entropy, or higher functional organization. But as this process of growth and development goes on, it will tend at various times to reach a limiting point; and will eventually reach a final end-point beyond which it will be difficult or impossible to find new and fruitful combinations. Living things are very elastic and adaptable, so that this end-point may be again and again postponed; but its approach will be constantly imminent once the warning signs have appeared.

In literary forms, "viability" — or life — means *interest*. So long as the new work is still interesting, it lives. When the possibilities of variation and innovation are exhausted, the work becomes possible, dull, it fails as literature. Works of literature, and literary forms, therefore develop constantly and grow — they seek new forms and new mixtures of subject matter — in order to remain interesting. When this ceases to be possible, they die.

(The best and clearest areas in which to study the process of hypertrophy are the history of chess, and the history of music. But hypertrophy is also the key to social development, and to the crises and catastrophes that afflict society and civilization. It's also an aspect of education: the turbulence of the 1960's was an example of hypertrophy — unbearable boredom — in the classroom, and unbearable organization in the universities.)

Now, the history of the sonnet is a neat study in hypertrophy; it has gone through several stages of dying and recovery. "Death and Resurrection" would be a good title for the history of the sonnet, divided into several episodes or cycles. At the present moment the sonnet is quite dead. It may be due for a brief resurrection at any time, I don't know, but it is now hardly breathing, buried underground somewhere. I don't say that Lampman killed it — in Canada he was the last remarkable exponent, and a very fine one. It died in his hands. Robert Finch, or Roy Daniells, may claim to have raised it from the dead, since then, but it only came up to a sitting position — and lay down again in their pages of pure homage to the form. One suspects that these good poets only visited the cemetery, out of respect, and say by the grave for awhile. Perhaps they saw a vision. But April is the cruellest month, for the sonnet.

The period of birth and of authentic life for the English sonnet occurred, as we know, in the last decade of the sixteenth century. It had had a sort of *still birth* earlier, owing to the joint labours of Wyatt and Surrey, but the true Elizabethan sonnet came from a distinguished father, one who is still renowned as a lover and a gentleman. Sir Philip Sidney, whose sequence *Astrophel and Stella* set the sonnet craze going in 1591, found the form so new and refreshing that he could ask —

> How falls it then that with so smooth an ease
> My thoughts I speak?...

The answer is plain. When the form is new it always seems somehow smooth and easy. The English got the sonnet from Petrarch and Dante; in Italian, *sonetto*, a small sound, was a little song: at first any short song would be called a sonnet. Today, a sonnet suggests, not a song, but a heavy, dull, leaden block of words — an old-fashioned sturdy chunk of well-nigh meaningless poetry. This is the result of history, of the accumulation of dead matter that was so often poured into the sonnet — in other words, the consequence of hypertrophy.

And yet it is to the Elizabethan sonnet that Lampman harks back, to the first sweet youth of the form:

> My lady is not learned in many books
> Nor hath much love for grave discourses, strung
> With gaudy ornament...

This, from "The Growth of Love," a short sequence of twelve sonnets for his wife — written in the early time of their romance — has all the trappings of Elizabethan love poetry, derived from Provençal and Italian tradition, and filtered through Keats and Rossetti. For this is always true when a literary form "dies", that it becomes the subject of imitation and occasional "re-birth" in later times — sometimes the model for stuffed owls and closet drama, as in the case of Elizabethan tragedy — sometimes for beautiful re-creation, as in the Pre-Raphaelite poetry from which Lampman, Carman and Roberts took their cue — but it is never again as fresh and free as it was in the beginning. At the very best it's a case of 'bringing new life to an old form' — but the old form wants to lie down and die. It is never the same as the new form, the true form, created to fit the present time.

The sonnet already began to die, to be exhausted of its first, best possibilities, by the middle of the 1590's. It had just four or five years of superb youthful energy; but still it had a lot of life in it, and it kept going for decades, with various renewals and transfusions, though never again with the excitement of first invention. In the 1590's even mediocre poets somehow wrote beautiful sonnets; everyone could write something pleasant to read. Lampman's sonnets, on the other hand, are no worse than other dull sonnets of his time — in fact, better — but they are not superb original poetry. He was not breaking new ground.

The point to notice here is how voracious the contemporaries of a new form can be to exploit its possibilities at once and to exhaust the form as far as they can. Consider what Shakespeare and his confrères did to the blank-verse play; what Dryden and Pope did to the heroic couplet in a short time; what Balzac and Dickens did to the novel; and in our time, what a few decades have done to free verse! A great artist who comes upon a new form wants to explore all the possibilities of that form right there and then — like a lion, he leaves almost nothing for anyone else. The excitement of one generation can exhaust any literary form or development; some total renovation is necessary to keep things going.

By 1954, Michael Drayton could write that "sonnets thus in bundles are impressed, / And ev'ry drudge doth dull our satiate ear." And John Donne, a little later, is so tired of the business that he can say, "He is a fool which cannot make one Sonnet, and he is mad which makes two."

Of great importance to Lampman, then, was what happened to the sonnet when it began to show signs of hypertrophy, because this kind of sciatica or arthritis is the same that appears in his poetry when he imitates these forms. The first heaps of sonnets in English were love sequences; and if this was played out then the exhaustion of the love theme has a profound significance. The Elizabethan love sonnet was infused by a kind of spirituality — almost a religion of love — that was derivative and short-lived. Much has been written about the love ideal, its origin in the Provence, its energy derived from the Virgin (the "-dynamo" of Dantean and Petrarchan sonnets), and its power as a source of beauty and elevation in the early poetry. Also, that a kind of counterpoint, or downgoing, to the hard-headed realities, as in Donne's early poetry, or Shakespeare's "My mistress' eyes are nothing like the sun" — announces the coming destruction of this ideal.

This is why Lampman's "Growth of Love" sequence is so intolerable, with its mixture of masked eroticism and borrowed idealism; why it is his most embarrassing failure in the sonnet form. Also, why the "Portrait of Six Sonnets," written for Katherine Waddell, is so much better, so much more real. In the first sequence, the "child-sweet mouth," the "innocent lips," the "child's wild air," almost suggest an attack of paedophilia; while in the second sequence, "that full pale brow," "the serious word," "the strength of woman's years," and phrases like "grey-eyed, for grey is wisdom," or "an honored form and face," suggest a more austere, un-idealized reality.

As the love-sonnet sequence began to pall, in Elizabethan times, the principal of hypertrophy demanded a new topic, a new tone, a new source of inspiration. This came with the religious sonnet sequence, as the poets turned from love to a higher sphere. A certain Henry Lok, in his *Sundry Christian Passions*, in 1597, seems to have been the first to adapt the form to this purpose. William Alabaster's *Divine Meditations*, John Donne's *Holy Sonnets*, and George Herbert's *The Temple* are the best-known sequences of this kind. But faith of the sort we see there did not outlive the seventeenth century: T.S. Eliot felt a profound nostalgia for the wholeness of belief that we find in this poetry. That belief was swallowed up by Cartesianism, Newtonianism, the lecherous Restoration, the reasonable eighteenth century, and the shattering scepticism of Hobbes, Voltaire, Hume and Gibbon. And then after two hundred years it was reborn as romantic pantheism, a mysterious, moving, searching poetry of nature — the kind of religion that Lampman inherited.

We will take that up again a bit later. But already in the seventeenth century, with the turmoil of political overthrow — the Diggers, the Levellers (Communists of those days), and Oliver Cromwell setting up democracy in religion — the sonnet had also become political. Lampman's political sonnets, those sonnets of invective and realistic social comment, owe much to Wordsworth; but they also go back to Milton, the first great model, who rhymes "frogs," "dogs" and "hogs," in the sonnet beginning "I did but prompt the age to quit their clogs..." Unfortunately, how unpoetical political poetry of this kind can be was already clear from the beginning. It is high-mindedness of a groaning, grumpy, discontented kind. More of a problem — of how to deal with the human lot, the actualities of things — than a discovery of new poetry. Anyhow, the sonnet received a temporary lift from politics.

There were almost no sonnets at all written in the period from 1680 to 1740, so we see that the death of the sonnet might really occur in earnest. Rhyming couplets don't mix well with sonnet rhyme schemes, in fact not at all. And yet Archibald Lampman has a sonnet completely done in couplets — probably a desperate attempt to bring life to the old form. (His sonnet is called "Man's Future," but it's certainly not the sonnet's future.)

Such sonnets as there are, between the time of Charles Cotton and William Cowper, are of an extremely brittle prosaic kind. They suffer from the blight of common sense, which now afflicts us all, and which certainly afflicted Lampman, though he is not influenced by any sonnets from this period. All you need to do is read a few sonnets from the eighteenth century, or from the Restoration period, to realize how thoroughly Lampman is attached to the Elizabethan aesthetic, and how closely the Romantic sonnet tried to return to the period of its first flowering.

The one kind of sonnet that is missing from Lampman's repertoire is what we might call *the friendly sonnet*, a sonnet written in a casual everyday voice, addressed to a friend on some ordinary occasion. Something like William Cowper's sonnet "To William Hayley, Esq.":

> Dear architect of fine Chateaux en l'air
> Worthier to stand forever, if they could...

Or Sir Samuel Egerton Brydges' "To Miss M —, Written by Moonlight, July 18, 1782":

> Sweet gentle angel, not that I aspire
> To win thy favour, though ambition raise
> My wishes high...

Or William Bowles' "To a Friend":

> Go, then, and join the murmuring city's throng!
> Me thou dost leave to solitude and tears...

The personal tone and the personal address, in this light style, do not occur in Lampman's sonnets, although one sonnet, "The Dog," at least comes near to it. Lampman's sonnets are for the most part generalized, impersonal, and although written in a very natural voice, pitched on a level of moral elevation and high thinking.

And this is the nub of the matter. It bears on the content problem in the hypertrophy of the sonnet, the set of moral and philosophic notions to which Lampman was deeply attached, in which he was imprisoned, one might say, by the age and the time in which he wrote. For, after all, what are these sonnets about? They are not mainly about love, not mainly about politics, not mainly about religion, but about that variant of religious emotion which we call Romanticism, and which finds its expression through the correlatives of nature. In the sonnets, Lampman is

44

continually asserting a kind of higher wisdom. What is his purpose? And what is the aim of this wisdom?

"This life is a depressing compromise," he says at the opening of one sonnet. And true enough, most human lives are torn between desire and compromise (disappointment, disillusion, pain, anguish, meaningless drift). But at a number of high points in human history we find the belief — or is it an illusion — that a mode of thinking is available to man, whereby he can find peace, harmony, serenity of mind and inward happiness. This was offered by Lao Tse in the *Tao Te Ching*, by Confucius in the philosophy of the just mean, by the Greek philosophers in the doctrine that virtue and knowledge are the key to inner harmony and true happiness, and by the Christian and other world religions in which salvation is found through faith. (A "kingdom of heaven within you" can be obtained through belief and love). These are high thoughts. I bring them up, because the central meaning of Wordsworth's poetry was just this kind of contemplative or experiential harmony, achieved through contact with nature. This idea is at the heart of Romanticism, and it is what Lampman deeply believed in toward the end of the nineteenth century, what he mainly tried to convey through the sententious mode of the sonnet as a vehicle of wisdom.

> Even as I watched the daylight how it sped
> From noon till eve, and saw the light wind pass
> In long pale waves across the flashing grass,
> And heard through all my dreams, wherever led,
> The thin cicada singing overhead,
> I felt what joyance all this nature has,
> And saw myself made clear as in a glass,
> How that my soul was for the most part dead.
> O light, I cried, and heaven, with all your blue,
> O earth, with all your sunny fruitfulness,
> And ye, tall lilies, of the wind-vexed field,
> What power and beauty life indeed might yield,
> Could we but cast away its conscious stress,
> Simple of heart becoming even as you.

A moment's thought, however, will tell us that this kind of redeeming wisdom — a state of transcendent harmony achieved through right thinking — has not been the way of poetry in the first half of the twentieth century. The external world impinging on the mind, in a negative disrupting manner, and the inner conflicts of the mind, torn by doubts and confusions, have given us the poetry called modern —

> The age demanded an image
> Of its accelerated grimace...

"The Waste Land," "The Second Coming," "The Age of Anxiety," — these are the keynote poems of the first fifty years of this century. It is only within the past fifteen years or so that there has again appeared in literature — against the terrible undertow of "confessional poetry" — a doctrine seeking serenity and spiritual harmony in poetry. But this has

45

been mainly through the influence of Eastern religion, Zen Buddhism, meditation, Yoga practice, and a philosophy of non-attachment. The shift to the twentieth century was away from such healing wisdom, away from the moral and spiritual panaceas of the Victorians, to uncompromising awareness and to the recording of discord in society and the individual.

Lampman was caught in the transition and divided by it. His mentor Arnold had begun a sonnet with the jagged line — "Who prop, thou ask'st, in these bad days, my mind?" — and answered by harking back to the Greeks, and to Sophocles, "Who saw life steadily, and saw it whole...."

George Meredith had undermined the ideal-love tradition with corrosive truth in his 16-line sonnet sequence *Modern Love* in 1862. Edwin Arlington Robinson had struck out with plain fact in a sonnet beginning—

> Because he was a butcher and thereby
> Did earn an honest living (and did right)....

And Thomas Hardy, in the sonnet "Hap," had questioned the entire cosmogony of optimism behing Romantic nature poetry:

> If but some vengeful god would call to me
> From up the sky and laugh....

But no god did laugh or answer. Robinson, in fact, writing in the same decade as Lampman, had suggested the implication of all this for the sonnet. He put his probing question indeed in a sonnet which is worth quoting entire:

> Oh for a poet — for a beacon bright
> To rift this changeless glimmer of dead grey;
> To spirit back the Muses, long astray,
> And flush Parnassus with a newer light;
> To put these little sonnet-men to flight
> Who fashion, in a shrewd mechanic way,
> Songs without souls, that flicker for a day,
> To vanish in irrevocable night.
>
> What does it mean, this barren age of ours?
> Here are the men, the women, and the flowers,
> The seasons, and the sunset, as before.
> What does it mean? Shall there not one arise
> To wrench one banner from the western skies,
> And mark it with his name forevermore?

The problem for Lampman, in other words, was that stated by Frost in the sonnet "The Oven Bird":

> The question that he frames in all but words
> Is what to make of a diminished thing.

After Lampman, sonnets are no longer in the mainstream of poetry. Around 1910, Ezra Pound, as a misguided college student, was writing a sonnet a day — but he later burned them all. In the transitional book *Ripostes*, he has a sonnet of 1911, which is a parody of the noble form and the noble thought:

> When I behold how black, immortal ink
> Drips from my deathless pen — ah, well-away!
> Why should we stop at all for what I think?...

Lampman in the 90's, however, was still planning a book to be entitled "A Century of Sonnets." It never appeared. There are actually 153 sonnets in Lampman's published work — and we know that the published work includes only about 65% of all he wrote — so that more sonnets are probably buried in the manuscripts. ("A Century of Sonnets," incidentally, is an Elizabethanism: in 1595 Barnabe Barnes published *A Divine Century of Spiritual Sonnets*. The word *century* meant a hundred of anything. But Lampman may have got his title from Browning —

> Rafael made a century of sonnets,
> Made and wrote them in a certain volume...

Most of the Lampman sonnets are written in the high old style, but he is aware of the need for innovation. Hypertrophy has him by the gills. In the Italian sonnet it's usually the sestet that permits of novelty in the rhyme-scheme. (This is Lampman's preferred form, abba abba plus sestet; occasionally there is a sonnet with the English rhyme-scheme, three quatrains and a couplet and the late "Portrait in Six Sonnets" is in this English form.) You do not begin to enjoy his sonnets until you see the game of variations — escaping hypertrophy — that he plays in the rhyme-scheme of the sestet. He tries practically every variation and combination possible, and he makes the sense accord with the advantage of the rhyme positions. More than this, he has some very odd experiments: a sonnet in couplets, as mentioned before, which is also inverted, the sestet preceding the octet. Also a sonnet of thirteen lines, starting with a truncated octet — abbaacc (which makes a very good verse). This is the sonnet "Fair Speech" (there are, by the way, two misprints in the punctuation in the printed version, in lines 7 and 8). There is a sonnet divided into seven and seven. There is one divided at the ninth line. There is a very effective couplet at the *beginning* of a sestet instead of at the close, in the poem "Thamyris". There are all kinds of exciting technical experiments.

But all these experiments are relatively conservative when compared with what had to be done to break through the hypertrophy of the form. Both the structure and the thought had to be radically shattered, and Lampman was not yet ready for this. I believed at one time that his political sonnets came nearest to making a breakthrough; and they certainly do point to the future, but they are still in the abstract ranting style of Milton and Wordsworth's political sonnets. What was needed you can see if you compare Gerard Manley Hopkins' sonnet "The World is Charged with the Grandeur of God", wrritten earlier than Lampman; or Yeats' sonnet "Leda and the Swan," which most people do not even recognize as a sonnet; or Cummings' fragmented and disguised sonnets; or Auden's "Sir, no man's enemy" and "Who's Who"; or Dylan Thomas' series "Altarwise by Owl-light" — a flow of hysterical mad verbiage completely outside the range of reason, sanity, or wisdom.

The closest Lampman comes to breaking through to a new intellectual position is in a sonnet like "Voices of Earth". Here an utter sense of unknowing is pushed to the brink of a far and austere faith, to things that were "before the making of the world":

> We have not heard the music of the spheres,
> The song of star to star, but there are sounds
> More deep than human joy and human tears,
> That Nature uses in her common rounds;
> The fall of streams, the cry of winds that strain
> The oak, the roaring of the sea's surge, might
> Of thunder breaking afar off, or rain
> That falls by minutes in the summer night.
> These are the voices of earth's secret soul,
> Uttering the mystery from which she came.
> To him who hears them grief beyond control,
> Or joy inscrutable without a name,
> Wakes in his heart thoughts bedded there, impearled,
> Before the birth and making of the world.

In the twentieth century some poets have written sonnets, obviously — but sonnets only in quotation marks. The form has been shattered beyond recognition. Only a few peripheral poets have held on to the sonnet, as drowning men hold on to a life-belt from the old ship: John Crowe Ransom, Ivor Winters, Allen Tate, Robert Graves — are traditional sonneteers. Dr. Merrill More, a psychiatrist, actually wrote two to five sonnets a day for a long period of years, but this is obviously a "psychiatric case" — he is said to have had a "compulsive addiction" to the sonnet. In any case, his sonnets are factual, flat, sane, modern day poems. Others, Richard Wilbur, W.D. Snodgrass, Donald Hall, may continue writing sonnets; but again we can see that this is a very special group, an oxbow of conservationists, if not conservatives. John Berryman was also a vigorous sonneteer — but then he was drunk, crazy, and in love at the same time. Only Lampman lives, because we are in Canada — all mild conservationists, if not conservatives — and because we want to sustain the great tradition, at least for a day or two. His achievement in the sonnet was utterly genuine, a continuation of all the best lines of sonnet writing throughout history; and his sonnets are in fact the best part of his work, the most solid and the most convincing. Nevertheless, he was butting against the tide; he struggled hard to assert the affirmative voice at a time when it was already most difficult to do so. Both his ideas and his structures show signs of the strain. They are a kind of bulwark against the flooding in of the twentieth century.

LOUIS K. MACKENDRICK

SWEET PATIENCE AND HER GUEST, REALITY:
The Sonnets of Archibald Lampman

My title comes from the sonnet "To the Warbling Vireo":

> Sweet little prattler, whom the morning sun
> Found singing, and this livelong summer day
> Keeps warbling still: here have I dreamed away
> Two bright band happy hours, that passed like one,
> Lulled by thy silvery converse, just begun
> And never ended. Thou dost preach to me
> Sweet patience and her guest, reality,
> The sense of days, and weeks, and months that run
> Scarce altering in their round of happiness,
> And quiet thoughts, and toils that do not kill,
> And homely pastimes. Though the old distress
> Loom gray above us both at times, ah, still,
> Be constant to thy woodland note, sweet bird;
> By me at least thou shalt be loved and heard.

This poem, not a particularly memorable or dramatic one, epitomises several characteristic attitudes and themes of Lampman in the form. There is the idea of certain natural endurances as distinct from the constancy of human woe (or perhaps the constancy of unregenerate human nature). Further, here as elsewhere the solitary or isolated poet prefers to stop and meditate in one of two usual manners: a rhetorical, abstract, or uplifting spirituality, or an intense focus on natural detail, objective presentation without any straining after "meaning" or "significance." Both contemplative moods or modes have singular elements of stasis, almost at times of paralysis; yet often in Lampman's sonnets we see a deliberate dichotomy between active and passive, noise and hush, thinking and intuiting, nature's beauty and the absence of such in men's lives, visualisation and impressionism. These contraries are generally un-resolved in the poet's attitude of absorption or possession.

To be specific, "patience" is stasis and uncritical acceptance; the guest, "reality", is both a Keatsian note of mortality and the highly crafted, selective, and detailed observation and rendering of the natural here-and-now. Sweet patience leads to Lampman's "dream," a concept which has been variously defined and which recurs almost obsessively in the sonnets; it is less often a vision, a reminiscence, than it is an attitude of reverie, a surrender to impressionism, sensuousness, or rhetoric (what Arthur L. Phelps has called the sometimes "mawkishly sentimen-tal, sometimes philosophically trite").[1]

This is borne out considerably in what Lampman had to say about the sonnet, particularly in his contributions to *At the Mermaid Inn*. The difficulty here is the frequently idealistic vagueness of his prescriptive pronouncements, and the occasional dogmatism: "Every man who writes verse at all must write a sonnet." He protested those "ex-asperatingly numerous" people who "profane and misapply the sonnet" and ironically cited his own "Falling Aslepp" as an instance of the un-suitability of the form to its small, homely subject. On behalf of the son-net Lampman spoke for such qualities as the gift of versification, true thought and feeling, the union of austere dignity and lyric fervour, a slight access of ruggedness, the accent of real tenderness or the freedom of the noblest beauty, simplicity, a patient ear, and majestic self-restraint.[2] The sonnet, then, is defined by Lampman both specifically and sublimely — the latter a tone in perhaps half his sonnets — in a pleasant ambivalence that John Marshall, his severest critic, attacked in 1901 in persuasive and unsparing detail.[3] However, Lampman was a per-former, not a theoretician.

Early criticism of the sonnets rarely considered matters of techni-que, relying instead upon an automatic response of readers to catchwords of emotional and transcendant quality, to an appreciation of rhetoric, not analysis. But there were a few less sweeping observations about the *how* of these poems, as opposed to their content, occasions when manner preceded matter. Louis Untermeyer, for instance, writing in 1909, remarked Lampman's "complete mastery of the subtlest technical nuances":

> Repetitions of phrases and their alternatives, skilful balancing of similar sounding words, and the varied use of accented rhythms tended to give many of his sonnets more actual melody than one usually finds in widely heralded 'songs.'[4]

Bernard Muddiman noted the "minute method of piling up details" and "the exactness, too, of the natural imagery."[5] G.H. Unwin also began to specify:

> Many of Lampman's sonnets are masterpieces of construction and phrasing, striking the happy mean between the severe and the ornamental style, with just enough of the poet's own thoughts to give them a personal value to the reader.[6]

50

Or again, from Raymond Knister in 1927,

> Crisp, apparently bare sentences build a firm structure, a clear picture, a moment of emotional realization.... In pictorial quality these sonnets remind one of clear water-colours, and the even excellence of picture in like number and quality seldom has been equalled.[7]

Over half of Lampman's published poems are sonnets. There are at least 115 individual poems and nine sequences of from two to ten sonnets, making a minimum of 150; this figure does not include those never reprinted in Duncan Campbell Scott's collections. It is well-known that Lampman considered the sonnets his best work. Though his points of view do become familiar, what counters this is the variety of things beheld or advocated and his technical competence.

By recent count, Lampman used fifty-four sonnet forms, nearly eighty per cent of which were employed only *once*, playing virtually mathematical permutations upon the sestet and using anywhere from four to seven rhymes in any such poem. The sonnets frequently, but not absolutely, divide into the conventional octave-sestet arrangement; conversely, though his favored form was the Shakespearian, he was in no way restricted to the quatrain sequence. Next in frequency was a variation on the Petrarchan octave, abbaacca; but in the nine forms which appear most regularly, from four to eighteen times, the last six lines have this interesting variety: efefgg, dedeff, defdef cdcdcd, ddeffe, dedfef, ddefef, deefdf, and cdeedc. As E.K. Brown has written,

> He has no constant or usual sonnet-form: sometimes he uses octave and sestet, sometimes he prefers quatrains and couplet; in his octaves he usually has three rhymes...although in some of his finest sonnets he restricts himself to the statutory two; he likes to set his couplet between the second and third quatrain, rather than at the close of the poem, but this liking is not consistent. Since he also likes to introduce his sestet with a couplet, the close reader growns to expect that the ninth and tenth lines of a Lampman sonnet...will form a rhyming interlude.[8]

Lampman's rhymes were usually exact, though there are some arresting instances of half-rhyme ("Solitude"). He had an extraordinary versatility in technique, and here a *caveat* by I.A. Richards in his *Practical Criticism* is appropriate, as he considered one of the chief difficulties in criticism, the effects of "technical presuppositions".

> When something has once been well done in a certain fashion we tend to expect similar things to be done in the future in the same fashion, and are disappointed or do not recognise them if they are done differently. Conversely, a technique which has shown its ineptitude for one purpose tends to become discredited for all. Both are cases of mistaking means for ends.... [Technical presuppositions] interfere whenever we make the mistake of supposing either that the *means* a poet uses are valuable for their own sake, or that they can be prescribed without reference to his aim, so that by mere inquiry into the means we can conclude as to the value.... The frequency and variety of these dogmatic pronouncements upon detail, irrespective of the final result, are amply [demonstrable].... Technical presuppositions, as a rule, are not products of reflection.[9]

It is manifestly inappropriate to tax Lampman with the technical models he may have used as his bases. As he wrote to E.W. Thomson in 1895, while proofreading *Lyrics of Earth,*

> Touching my sonnets I am very much comforted by your approval. Some of the cases of extra feet in the lines which you point out need correction: one or two of them I regret to say I have left there intentionally for the effect seemed to me good and I have no very profound respect for rules and regulations.[10]

Another technical matter in the sonnets is Lampman's deployment of sounds, both in the sense of how lines of poetry are heard and in the frequent choice of natural or human auditory values as subjects. A study of these showns many sonnets to be carefully structured, but more so in the nature poems than in those of political, social, ideological, ethical, admonitory, or rhetorical substance. Lampman's alliterative qualities are, when not completely obvious and uncontributory, remarkably subtle. However, they become lost in poems which are catalogues or in those in which assonantal sounds are prominent, which is usual. It is the latter that are managed with delicacy, consistency, and a colloquially low profile.

The conjunction of sound and sense is infrequent, even when sounds are a sonnet's subject, but the occasional coincidence is remarkable. Such is the case of "The Railway Station," in which sharp vowels and abrupt, harsh sounds properly complement the subject. These are succeeded by less stringent words befitting the observer's turn to meditation; the same sounds are used, but the new context transforms their onomatopoeic quality. Again, from the first sonnet of "New Year's Eve,"

> I saw as in the flashing of a vision,
> Far down between the tall towers of the night,
> Borne by great winds in awful unison,
> The teeming masses of mankind sweep by
> Even as a glittering river with deep sound....

the repeated vowel sounds long and short "a", long "e", long and short "i", and umlaut "a" unify the lines, and effectively parallel the drawn-out procession of suffering mankind. (See also "A Thunderstorm" and "The March of Winter," below.) In g"on Lake Temiscamingue,"

> A single dreamy elm, that stands between
> The sombre forest and the wan-lit lake,
> Halves with its slim gray stem and pendent green
> The shadowed point. Beyond it without break
> Bold browns of pine-topped granite bend away....

the same case obtains; the long and short "a", short "i", and long "e", though, have little apparent relation to what is described. There are many examples of similar sound effects, which usually occur in the sonnet's opening lines. The continuation and repetition of such sounds does not necessarily observe the strict proximity often associated with assonance; like Lampman's unhaphazard dispersal of terminal rhymes in the sonnet, they may and do enfilade the poem. It can be argued that vowels obviously recur massively in language, but this is language organised into poetry. We rarely perceive that Lampman at his best is very far away from colloquial ease, except when he indulges an unhappy fondness for romantic archaisms, syntactical inversions, and biblical forms of address.

Lampman reiterates certain ideas, attitudes, and themes throughout his sonnets, and in some he emphasizes perceptual keynotes or touchstones: these, too, recapitulate sweet patience and reality. As has been noted, dream and the posture of thoughtless meditation pervade the sonnets, as in "Love-Wonder": "...words and woven phrases fall to naught, / Lost in the silence of one dream divine." The rejection of the world of conscious thought is also put forward in "Music":

> Surely not painful ever, yet not glad,
> Shall such hours be to me, but blindly sweet,
> Sharp with all yearning and all fact at strife....

A kind of purely sensational responsiveness is evident here; Lampman lays claim to the validity of a thorough impressionism. This is supplemented with undemanding, inactive intuition; he is "Content only to listen and to know" in "To the Cricket," or, as in "Ambition,"

> For me, the dreamer, 'tis enough to know
> The lyric stress, the fervour sweet and wild;
> I sit me in the windy grass and grow
> As wise as age, as joyous as a child.

The natural impulse preempts the straining after and in thought. The same attitude appears in "An Old Lesson From the Fields":

> O earth, with all your sunny fruitfulness,
> And ye, tall lilies, of the wind-vexed field,
> What power and beauty life indeed might yield,
> Could we but cast away its conscious stress,
> Simple of heart becoming even as you.

Finally, "Aspiration" contrasts visionaries and earth-tied life, and suggests that aspiration and dreaming provide equal satisfaction and opening of the senses: the dream is necessary to bearing with life.

What has to be borne is the other side of life, mankind (in E.E. Cummings' word, "manunkind"). In "Love-Doubt" the reflective personality characterizes himself as "with dreams weighed, that ever heard / Sad burdens echoing through the loudest throng," or, in "Knowledge,"

> Oh for a life of leisure and broad hours,·
> To think and dream, to put away small things,
> This world's perpetual leaguer of dull naughts...

53

The wish acquires the force of obsession through repetition in the sonnets, as in "In the Pine Groves", where the poet sees himself "With a soul shaped to its accustomed load / Of silly cares and microscopic dreams...." Lampman's desire is

> ...to keep the mind at brood
> On life's deep meaning, nature's altitude
> Of loveliness, and time's mysterious ways ("Outlook")

because

> Only the things of Beauty shall endure.
> While man goes woeful, wasting his brief day,
> From Truth and Love and Nature far astray,
> Lo! Beauty, the lost goal, the unsought cure.... ("Beauty")

Or there is "Night," when Lampman feels himself "once more a soul self-cognizant and still": he avoids the pettinesses of day, almost a rationalisation for not facing, or being paranoiacally discouraged by, the daylight world.

In his sonnets Lampman was particularly mordant about human society and its institutions, and his poetic opinions, when more than simply disapproving, show directly why much of his verse was devoted to the natural world. Even in his Grecian Urn, "The Frogs," man and his cities are subject to time and death. The former bears down inexorably in "Despondency," where

> life doth seem,
> Save for the certain nearness of its woes,
> Vain and phantasmal as a sick man's dream

— an intriguing paradox, that the only thing making life less spectral is its woes, the only summons to living. "A Night of Storm" dramatises the arch-foe, the city, where men make and meet "rude fates, hard hearts, and prisoning poverty," while in "The Railway Station" the train is virtually a metaphor of the pain in human life. Even in the less specific "New Year's Eve" mankind is a self-warring, self-defeating species, intolerant and vicious, and in the ironically titled "Gentleness" the sonnet's rhetorical weight is directed towards man's blind strife, self-engendered misery, pride, malice, self-will, greed, and blind-voiced anger. A complementary situation is found in "To A Millionaire", where the poet considers

> the unnumbered broken hearts,
> The hunger and the mortal strife for bread,
> Old age and youth alike mistaught, misfed,
> By want and rags and homelessness made vile....

Again, and finally, "The True Life," like many of Lampman's ethical sonnets, gives much proportionate time to the opposite of what is prescribed; here life is a

> depressing compromise
> Between the soul and what it wills to do
> And what your careful neighbours plan for you...

Little man's world has the potential for joy and strength

> Could we but sweep forever from our path
> Your cant rules and detested casuistries,
> Your clap-trap, and your damned hypocrisies.

Little wonder, then, that Nature became for Lampman, in archetypal Romantic fashion, a place where large eternal matters, not human tininesses, could be absorbed, not thought upon. As he wrote in 1892,

> The happiest man is he who has cultivated to the utmost the sense of beauty. The man who is able at all times to find perfect and prolonged satisfaction in the contemplation of a tree, a field, a flower or a 'spear of grass,' can never be bored save by his fellow-creatures.[11]

Before I consider those Lampman sonnets which are good by any standards, there are several instances of note where a fine expression seems totally self-sufficient poetically, occasionally to the near redemption of an otherwise indifferent poem.[12] Forr example, the phrase cited above from "Outlook," "nature's altitude / Of loveliness," is itself lovely; coming within the inspirational note of the sonnet, it is an ineffable concept put with un usual precision. Again, Lampman's two-sided people, "The Poets," are "Poor shining angels, whom the hoofs betray, / Whose pinions frighten with their goatish smell," and these vividly immediate images save the poem from being merely a catalogue of equal and opposite qualities. In "At Dusk" there are the splendid visual and auditory values of

> ...now the whip-poor-will,
> Beyond the river margins glassed and thinned
> Whips the cool hollows with his liquid note

as Lampman goes beyond objective description into sheer metaphorical notation. "Storm Voices," dramatically elaborating a vague precursor, "Voices of Earth," has powerful images — "There is a surging horror in the night; / The woods far out are roaring in their might" — in an interesting psychological study; the images are reinforced by the lines' sounds. Or, finally, from "The Modern Politican," an astringent and bitter piece of invective:

> Now comes the transit age, the age of brass,
> When clowns into the vacant empires pass...
> So that they glitter, each his little day,
> The little mimic of a vanished king.

This is straightforward address, metaphorically rich, colloquial and strong, and brutally affective: powerful feelings are poetically disciplined.

[In considering Lampman's outstanding sonnets and the categories they suggest, it will be evident that I react differently to Louis Dudek's approval of the "direct declarative sonnets, patterned on Milton and Wordsworth, expressing moral indignation, intellectual conflict, a noble struggle with the world," though he rightly sees many of the nature poems as escapist, refugist, pastoral, inaccurate, and as romantic dreams.[13] Lampman's best sonnets contain many characteristic styles and concerns. In "Solitude," for instance, Munro Beattie has noted that "Successive sounds seem to mark off areas of silence in a scale of increasing intensity."[14]

> Sometimes a hawk screams or a woodpecker
> Startles the stillness from its fixèd mood
> With his loud careless tap. Sometimes I hear
> The dreamy white-throat from some far off tree
> Pipe slowly on the listening solitude,
> His five pure notes succeeding pensively.

These sounds, sharp or muffled, also have a high power of visual suggestion. The details are undemonstrative and objective; there is no attempt to affect the reader emotionally or rhetorically. There is a progression from stillness to a relative peaking of sounds, followed by a balance or resolution of these — as Sandra Djwa has said, "a series of associations tied together by natural sequence."[15] The poet's situation is characteristically still, as it is in "The Frogs", in the warm noontime fixity of "Before the Robin," and in the once abruptly interrupted silence of "A Forest Path in Winter." The equivalent mental attitude appears in the immobile, watchful, mute control of "Comfort," in the paralysed reaction of the speaker of "Despondency," and in "Perfect Love," where a lover reacts only silently to his awareness of her life and action, his passive quiescence.]

Lampman often makes fine use of visual perspective; a model here among the sonnets is "Across the Pea-Fields." The poem begins by seeing fields in the middle distance, advances beyond the city to the hill-packed horizon, and then reverses to the viewer's immediate vicinity. Here is a familiar Lampman note of haze and blurring, a variation of the celebrated "Heat." The same is true of "A Niagara Landscape," varying perspectives in mid-day indistinctness, and of "Winter Uplands," where the clarity of atmosphere complements the several distinct foci as the poetic lens finally settles on a constellation. But it is "A Dawn on the Lièvre" which has the most memorable development.

> Up the dark-valleyed river stroke by stroke
> We drove the water from the rustling blade;
> And when the night was almost gone we made
> The Oxbow bend; and there the dawn awoke;

Full on the shrouded night-charged river broke
The sun, down the long mountain valley rolled,
A sudden swinging avalanche of gold,
Through mists that sprang and reeled aside like smoke.
And lo! before us, toward the east upborne,
Packed with curled forest, bunched and topped with pine,
Brow beyond brow, drawn deep with shade and shine,
The mount; upon whose golden sunward side,
Still threaded with the melting mist, the morn
Sat like some glowing conqueror satisfied.

Apart from the predominance of certain lingering sounds in the sonnet's language, here is an unravelling of qualities and intensities of light as the eye moves upwards from river level to sun-broken misty peaks, from semi-darkness to vivid glow. The ascent of the poet's sight, interrupted by a contrary downward movement, is paralleled by the growing clarity of detail and a resolution in an appropriate simile. The same sense of *process* is apparent in "In November," as "The hills and leafless forest slowly yield / To the thick-driving snow," in "Evening," with its seeing and hearing from dusk to dark, and in "After Mist."

Lampman used poetic analogy — metaphor and simile — sparingly, but thoughtfully. "A Thunderstorm" is a fine sonnet with its metaphor of military attack and its discerning sound effects.

A moment the wild swallows like a flight
Of withered gust-caught leaves, serenely high,
Toss in the windrack up the muttering sky.
The leaves hang still. Above the weird twilight,
The hurrying centres of the storm unite
And spreading with huge trunk and rolling fringe,
Each wheeled upon its own tremendous hinge,
Tower darkening on. And now from heaven's height,
With the long roar of elm-trees swept and swayed,
And pelted waters, on the vanished plain
Plunges the blast. Behind the wild white flash
That splits abroad the pealing thunder-crash,
Over bleared fields and gardens disarrayed,
Column on column comes the drenching rain.

There is an inherent tripartite division of sky, the connection of sky and earth in the transitional tree image, and ground, with ceaseless movement throughout. Metaphor is also central in "Goldenrod" in terms of harvest, in "A Night of Storm," where very specific imagery equates the storm with the city-dwellers it lashes, and in the sustaining water analogies of "Deeds", which give this sonnet a significant turn away from elementary didacticism. See also "The Passing of the Spirit": the wind in pines is a substantial image for an abstraction, man's sudden dreaming of his immortality. Finally, "The March of Winter" is an outstanding example of analogy.

They that have gone by forest paths shall hear
The outcry of worn reeds and leaves long shed,
The rise and sound of waters. Overhead,

Out of the wide northwest, wind-stripped and clear,
Like some great army dense with battle gear,
    All day the columned clouds come marching on,
    Long hastening lines in sombre unison,
Vanguard, and centre, and still deepening rear;
While from the waste beyond the barren verge
    Drives the great wind with hoof and thong set free,
And buffets and wields high its whistling scourge
    Around the roofs, or in tempestuous glee,
Over the far-off woods with tramp and surge,
    Huge and deep-tongued, goes roaring like the sea.

The extended simile is powerful, evocative, and threatening. The first three lines seem not to belong to the sonnet until Lampman's poetic logic becomes apparent: the "outcry" of reeds and leaves, otherwise a gratuitous pathetic fallacy, prepares for the tyrant's scourge, and the "sound of waters" anticipates the great wind as sea. It is also the poem's finale that forces reconsideration of the subtle sound-values throughout.

A related kind of sonnet is exemplified by "The Ruin of the year." Alter details of Autumn's mute waiting we have

And now the fall and all the slow soft ruin:
And soon some day comes by the pillaging wind,
The winter's wild outrider, with harsh roar,
And leaves the meadows sacked and waste and thinned,
And strips the forest of its golden store;
Till the grim tyrant comes, and then they sow
The silent wreckage, not with salt, but snow.

There is a logical development, progression, from gentle fading to vicious pillaging in the concluding personification, and a vigorous contrast between the apparently dreamy beginning and the savage, emphatic ending. The sonnet's time-schemes are obvious: the warning in the immediate moment, the seemingly distant past of summer and autumn, and the imminent levy of the conqueror winter. It is this kind of *development* that also exists in "Evening" and more particularly in "Indian Summer." Here an extended personification of a Lampman dreamer, highly reminiscent of Keats' "To Autumn," concludes in an apt strong contrast as the figure

Nor sees the polar armies overflood
The darkening barriers of the hills, nor hears
The north-wind ringing with a thousand spears.

Another example is "On Lake Temiscamingue"; again there is a perceptible change from the "shadowed point" to "A race of tumbled rocks, a roar of foam," from the observed passive to the active in Nature, and from the visual to the aural.

Desmond Pacey has written of Lampman's "double vision,"

This dynamic tension [of dream and nightmare] is present in all the best of his poetry; the substance of his thought is the ultimately unsuccessful attempt to cherish the dream and keep the nightmare at bay.[16]

Such a duality may be easily seen as the symbolic or dramatic tensions or polarities that inform most literature. This structural device is everywhere apparent in Lampman's sonnets, but there are particular and deliberate poems in which it is formal, not casual. "A January Morning" offers a good vivid opposition of hush and noise, of morning vision and the vigorous activity of the woodmen's early start. The sonnet is an illustration of sweet patience and reality as are any number of others: "To the Ottawa" carries both the specific and rhetorical, objective and romantic terms of address, while "Gentleness" sets an inspirational presentation of that quality against jarring mankind. "Love-Wonder" distinguishes saying and dream as a lover is content in "the beating wonder" of his thought rather than acting to word it, and "Night in the Wilderness" contrasts the familiar human level with a grim mysterious natural presence, the region of the campfire with the dark distances beyond.

Lampman was fond of lists, and the best of these in sonnet form are free from a summary moral. His last poem, "Winter Uplands," is a catalogue, adding detail to detail without comment, rather than having any sentimental or ethical overstatement. Inferences are at the reader's discretion; if he wishes to make a case in terms of theme, he must re-examine individual words and phrases. There are many sonnets like this one: "Nesting Time," "April Voices," "After the Shower," "At Dusk," all sights but for a sound conclusion, "The Passing of Spring," "Music," an impressionist record of the effects of another's playing, and "Dead Cities," a self-explanatory *ubi sunt* sequence.

A final grouping of sonnets, which take place in the sombre times or seasons that Lampman favored, has to do with the psychology of a speaker who may or may not be the poet. The measure of these is the deceptive "Winter Evening."

> To-night the very horses springing by
> Toss gold from whitened nostrils. In a dream
> The streets that narrow to the westward gleam
> Like rows of golden palaces; and high
> From all the crowded chimneys tower and die
> A thousand aureoles. Down in the west
> The brimming plains beneath the sunset rest,
> One burning sea of gold. Soon, soon shall fly
> The glorious vision, and the hours shall feel
> A mightier master; soon from height to height,
> With silence and the sharp unpitying stars,
> Stern creeping frosts, and winds that touch like steel,
> Out of the depth beyond the eastern bars,
> Glittering and still shall come the awful night.

The sonnet is carefully built up to the end of "awful night" by particular words, hints of endings and finalities in the golden twilight —

"whitened," "narrow," "die," "west," "burning" — all of which over-power the initial "dream." The poem begins mellowly but ends in a kind of horror which logically concludes a process of internalisation of the double-sided natural details. Again, in "A Summer Evening," there is a progression from characteristically objective observations of the hazy immediate environment, up to heaven, back down to the very local "grossip cricket", to this:

> Then night, the healer, with unnoticed breath,
> And sleep, dark sleep, so near, so like to death.

The poem begins and ends monosyllabically, in dying and dead sounds. It moves from observed things through their blurring (in natural terms) to eternity and the peaceful winding-down of day in another quiet shud-der. "A Summer Evening" is a carefully constructed sonnet with a dis-cernible poetic and psychological development, almost a telling-over of the familiar and a preparation for last things. Without radical distortion everything can be seen in symbolic terms as a psychological manifesta-tion of a growing mood, with a final transformation into mental and physical fading-out.

There are other like sonnets. "In Absence," a lover's meditation, wishes safety and uncomplicated rest for the loved one, but

> My love is far away and I am grown
> A very child, oppressed with formless glooms,
> Some shadowy sadness with a name unknown
> Haunts the chill twilight, and these silent rooms
> Seem with vague fears and dim regrets astir,
> Lonesome and strange and empty without her.

This is not a powerful poem, but it has a sombre mental logic: the speaker's change to sadness is implied by his mention of those generalised things that might disturb her rest. In surrogate fashion he takes on the "formless glooms" which he conjures up, which comple-ment his own loneliness and, perhaps, his psychological dependency upon her. "Storm Voices" features an interesting modification from ranting storm into the poet's private thoughts; the latter come in slow measures which radically alter the sonnet's pace and which are given religious terminology ("spirit," "holy," "organ thunders," "hymns," "cathedral gloom"). In the storm the speaker hears "strange human voices" and is possessed by a sad passion; the poem makes explicit the connection between Nature and the man. But it is the quality of the con-trast between outer chaos and inner melancholy that is psychologically significant here. Barrie Davies, to a somewhat like degree, has read the sonnet allegorically as the critical condition of the contemporary in-dividual, besieged by the forces of diminishment.[17]

Furthermore, in "Sorrow" we see a dramatic change from sleep's "sweet dream" to a waking remembrance of sorrow, as the poet is so lashed by unreasoning blindness to the new day that "Eaten by passion,

stripped of all my pride, / I wished that somehow then I might have died.
" The sonnet is kin to the masochistic experience given in Yeats' "The Cold Heaven." Finally, there is "The Autumn Waste," a uniformly dreary poem, sordid and unredeeming, haunted by images of death, uncharacteristically morbid and unlike Lampman: "Life, hopes, and human things seem wrapped away, / With shrouds and spectres, in one long decay." Something has interfered with his usual undemonstrative contemplation; the environment is a direct and convenient expression of some very dark matter in the viewer.

It has not been my purpose to place Lampman in or against a tradition of the sonnet, nor to measure him by grander practitioners, but simply to show what he does and how he does it. We may not suggest, as did Bernard Muddiman, that

> The peculiarly limited field of this form of verse was best suited for his mental strength. A solitary thought could be adorned in all its becoming glory. The slow movement of the surgent and resurgent wave of the sonnet kept admirable pace with the gait of his brain.[18]

Though meant favorably, the point now appears derogatory. Do we perhaps argue, as did Arthur L. Phelps, that Lampman was a good minor poet, and add that his talents were not of sufficient range or maturity to be continually novel, at best an improbable demand? I do not feel competent to determine if, in his sonnets, Lampman was a stylist or a mannerist. But it is too simplistic to conclude that these poems are facile or formulaic, even though expression, ideas, or points of view fall into what become patterns. Instances of what I have discussed multiply to a considerable degree; situations, attitudes, and techniques repeat themselves without giving the sense of purely mechanical accomplishment. There are sonnets by Lampman which are genuinely distinguished. Not all reward fine and specialised examination, few are replete with variant meanings, and none are difficult of access in terms of plain sense. Such minute investigative treatment will usually deform these poems and cloud his understated, apparent competency and achievements.

NOTES

[1] Arthur L. PHELPS, *Canadian Writers* (Toronto: McClelland & Stewart, 1951), 54.

[2] Arthur S. BOURINOT (ed.) *At the Mermaid Inn* (Ottawa: Arthur S. Bourinot, 1958), 55, 32, 56.

[3] John MARSHALL, "Archibald Lampman," in Michael GNAROWSKI (ed.), *Critical Views on Canadian Writers: Archibald Lampman* (Toronto: Ryerson, 1970), 33-54.

[4] Louis UNTERMEYER, "Archibald Lampman and the Sonnet" in GNAROWSKI, 57, 58.

[5] Bernard MUDDIMAN, "Archiblad Lampman," in GNAROWSKI, 71, 72.

[6] G.H. UUNWIN, "The Poetry of Archibald Lampman," in GNAROWSKI, 86-87.

[7] Raymond KNISTER, "The Poetry of Archibald Lampman," in GNAROWSKI, 117.

[8] E.K. BROWN, *On Canadian Poetry* (Toronto: Ryerson, 1944), 115-116. I will not be discussing what if any effect Lampman's disposition of rhyme has upon the idea-order of the sonnets.

[9] I.A. RICHARDS, *Practical Criticism* (New York: Harcourt, Brace, 1930), 16-17, 294, 294-95, 296.

[10] Arthur S. BOURINOT (ed.), *Archibald Lampman's Letters to Edward William Thomson* (Ottawa: Arthur S. Bourinot, 1956), 32.

[11] BOURINOT (ed.), *At the Mermaid Inn*, 35.

[12] Here I acknowledge the dangers of impressionism, to which Lampman and many of his commentators are susceptible.

[13] Louis DUDEK, "The Significance of Lampman," in GNAROWSKI, 196, 197.

[14] Munro BEATTIE, "Archibald Lampman," in *Our Living Tradition: Seven Canadians*, ed. Claude T. BISSELL (Toronto: University of Toronto Press, 1957), 83.

[15] Sandra DJWA, "Lampman's Fleeting, Vision," *Canadian Literature* 56 (Spring, 1973), 25.

[16] Desmond PACEY, *Ten Canadian Poets* (Toronto: Ryerson, 1958), 129.

[17] Barrie DAVIES, "Lampman and Religion," *Canadian Literature* 56 (Spring, 1973), 45.

[18] MUDDIMAN, 79-80.

DICK HARRISON

"SO DEATHLY SILENT":
The Resolution of Pain and Fear
in the Poetry of Lampman and D.C. Scott

Pain and fear are not the feelings we usually associate with the work of Lampman or Duncan Campbell Scott, but they are there in the poetry surprisingly often and in various forms. Scott's Indian characters suffer the direct, outward pain of the northern winter, or like the Half-Breed Girl, the anguish of being caught between two worlds. Lampman as poet suffers the "loneliness, perplexity and pain" of the city. Sandra Djwa tells us, in fact, that "Lampman's poetic vocabulary is often concerned with the negative emotions of 'pain', 'misery', 'fear', 'loneliness', 'loss', and 'emptiness'.[1] And if these negative emotions are not found at typical moments in the poetry, they do appear at moments of intensity, when we see some aspects of the poetry with unusual clarity. Partly because of their intensity, these moments also provide the sharpest contrasts between Lampman's and Scott's poetic worlds. The sources of pain and fear in their worlds and the ways of resolving them can tell us something about how those worlds differ.

The pain and fear we are concerned with here, it must be remembered, is that found in the poetic, as distinct from the private worlds of Lampman and Scott. The emergence of personal experience into poetry takes such oblique and unpredictable forms that it can only be safely examined in a much broader context. Witness the still unfinished debate about whether Lampman's life as an Ottawa civil servant did or did not give him a melancholy caste of mind. The intense personal pain Scott suffered at the sudden death of his daughter forced from him one unexceptionable poem, "The Closed Door," but its main effect as E. K. Brown tells us, was that Scott was virtually unable to write for four years.[2]

The usual source of pain and fear in Lampman's poetry is obviously mankind and its "strife" — a word which recurs in the poems. At its extreme this strife is aggressive and threatening, like "the horrible crash of the strong man's feet" ("Freedom") or the nightmare vision of "The City of the End of Things," but often it is simply cold and indifferent, like "the echoing city towers, / The blind gray streets, the jingle of the throng" in "Among the Timothy." The city, full of this meaningless and intrusive noise, is the embodiment of man's strife, as in the poem "The City."

> And toil hath fear for neighbour,
> Where singing lips are dumb,
> And life is one long labour
> Till death or freedom come.

The city imprisons man in an alien order, but Lampman is rarely a social critic in the sense of identifying the individual's woes with particular systems or institutions. The darkness that produces the fear is also in the human heart. In "April," for example, pain is a result of man's nature, or at least of what he has made of himself in the city. He suffers from "The shallow toil, the strife against the grain," but also because of "near souls, that hear us call, but answer not." In "A Night of Storm," the forces of violent nature, the indifferent city, and the fallen condition of man combine to produce an almost demonic picture of torment.

> More dark and strange thy veiled agony,
> City of storm, in whose gray heart are hidden
> What stormier woes, what lives that groan and beat,
> Stern and thin-cheeked, against time's heavier sleet,
> Rude fates, hard hearts, and prisoning poverty.

The storm with its "fierce winds" becomes in effect a tangible image of the painful turmoil of human life, the "veilèd agony."

It would be misleading to say that Lampman's poetry exhibits none of the pain and fear in nature found in Scott's. In "Winter" for example, "The wet woods moan: the dead leaves break and fall" at the coming of autumn. This sort of pain in nature should be distinguished from the "elegiac" tone Louis Dudek identifies in Lampman's nature descriptions.[3] That, it seems to me, Lampman inherits with the conventions of pastoral imagery he has taken, as Roberts and Carman did, from the English Romantics. The ideal state of man is to live in harmony with a beneficent, possibly divine, natural order. By its usual extension this same convention endorses Lampman's view of the city as corrupt and degenerate. Because the ideal state is unattainable except in fleeting transcendental moments of vision or "dream," that edenic condition must be ascribed to some remote, timeless age of innocence. The elegy is for that lost innocence (in effect, The Fall), and the metaphor of pastoral elegy has been read in that way at least since the eighteenth-century "Graveyard Poets," or Wordsworth's "Boy of Winander." It is a lament for lost innocent selves. In Lampman's own "A Child's Music Lesson," the poet says

> Toil on sweet hands; once more I see the child
> The little child, that was myself appears
> And all the old time beauties, undefiled,
> Shine back to me across the opening years.

The child is asked to toil on in the vain attempt to sustain what is necessarily fleeting. The lost selves are not usually this explicit, but the same elegiac tone invests all of Lampman's reflections upon man's lost innocence. In "Winter Store," for example, the poet relives his summer experiences of the divine beauty of nature or man-in-nature, but when he turns to the doings of mankind, the recognition that man cannot recapture that prelapsarian state comes to him with the intensity of "a passion and a cry," a "blind sorrow," a "nameless hunger of the soul." Hence the elegiac tone, though the poet is also sorrowing for himself as the poem ends:

> In vain, in vain,
> I remember how of old
> I saw the ruddy race of men,
> Through the glittering world outrolled,
>
> . . . .
>
> Treading in a wreathed line
> By a pathway through a wood.

The elements of pastoral harmony are there; the lament is for the lost perfection of man, but also for the loss of the poet's own ideal vision which he tries vainly to hold.

Beyond this largely conventional elegiac tone, some of Lampman's most intense images are of terror, pain, and grief in nature, like the image of the trees in "In October": "The sad trees rustle in chill misery, / A soft strange inner sound of pain-crazed lips." Here is a misery potentially more awful than the senseless rigours of the city because it seems passive, inward, and self-destructive. In "Autumn Waste," the image of "a lisping moan, an inarticulate cry, / Creeps far among the charnel solitudes," like the well-known "crying in the dark" of "Midnight" suggests a very haunting and pervasive suffering, a world-grief more appalling because its object is more undefined than the strife of men. Similar intensities appear in such poem as "Lament of the Winds," "Winter Evening," and "Storm Voices." But notice that the negative feelings are almost invariably associated with autumn, winter, or storm, times of the decay of living nature or its destruction by the harsher elements. At these times "Nature" herself is suffering, and unlike the suffering of mankind, hers has a purpose, is part of an enduring process. As we see in "Ballade of Summer's Sleep" or "Winter Hues Recalled," the winter is part of the passage to spring and can have its own beauties. Winter-grief is not a pain to be escaped, like the roar of the city, but a process in which man naturally participates. Lampman is not repelled by the pain of nature in "In October," but stays and gradually assumes the mood of the scene:

> Here I will wait a little; I am weary
> Not torn by pain of any lurid hue
> But only still and very gray and dreary,
> Sweet sombre land, like you.

By yielding himself to it the poet seems to resolve the impression of pain into a dull awareness of the necessary seasonal decay.

In Scott's poetry pain and fear are less likely to be the subject of a lyric outcry than the source of tension in a dramatic narrative. They are typically generated not by the strife of manking but by the environment with which man struggles, including the wild nature in which Lampman finds his solace from pain. In "Night Hymns on Lake Nipigon," the wilderness is a threatening and engulfing presence, as it is in "Rapids at Night," "At Gull Lake," and "The Flight." The typical reaction to this pain and fear is to fight, as the Indian mother does in "The Forsaken." This pattern at once emphasizes the difference between the sustained reflective moods of Lampman's poetry and the contrasts, tension, and violence in Scott's. Even his descriptive verse has a quality A. J. M. Smith has described as "dynamism."[4]

The most complete paradigm of the sources and resolution of pain and fear can be seen in "At Gull Lake, August 1810." The trader, Nairn, rejects Keejigo's love, and her pain is imaged in the wounded crane and the wolverine bleeding in a trap. When she returns to the expected vengeance of her husband, Tabashaw, repeating the words of a love song she has sung for Nairn, " 'Release the captive, / Heal the wound under the feathers,' " the lines evidently have an entirely changed meaning. She is seeking the pain which will release her totally.

On the surface, Keejigo's pain is man-made, but from the imagery of wolverine and crane it is clear that the cause is not Tabashaw or Nairn but the tragic division between her French and Indian blood, which leaves her a fit inhabitant of neither world. Characteristically, Scott does not treat her plight as a half-breed sociologically, as an injustice done to the Indian by the encroaching white culture, but philosophically, as one of the ways in which life cruelly betrays the helpless. The forces of this unkind universe are reinforced by the elements, in a violent storm which accompanies the rising climax of Keejigo's personal drama:

> Then burst the storm —
> The Indians' screams and the howls of the dogs
> Lost in the crash of hail
> That smashed the sedges and reeds,
> Stripped the poplars of leaves,
> Tore and blazed onwards,
> Wasting itself with riot and tumult —
> Supreme in the beauty of terror.

Nature is as violently divided against itself as the spirit of Keejigo. The phrase "the beauty of terror," repeated three times in the poem, expresses Scott's ambivalent attitude toward nature and toward the violence in which pain and fear can culminate. The struggle is traumatic, destructive, yet the forces which overwhelm man are grand, amoral, and aesthetically magnificent, like the storm in "Night Hymns" which "whelms" the singers in "splendid hollows of booming thunder." The effect in "At Gull Lake" is cathartic. After Keejigo, blinded and disfigured, resigns herself to a kind of death into nature, the moon rises, purged of all stain: "After the beauty of Terror the beauty of Peace."

Man does not ultimately overcome the threatening forces around him — even the valiant woman of "The Forsaken" does not. I would not even agree with Desmond Pacey, that out of the conflict beauty and peace necessarily emerge.[5] But the spirit is gloriously affirmed in the struggle. Scott is in this respect a forerunner of Pratt. In a late lyric, "At Sea," Scott compares a labouring, storm-bound ship with the soul of man:

> Sure only of battle and longing
>   Of the pain and the quest,
> And beyond in the darkness somewhere
>   Sure of her rest.

The darkness is not dispelled, but the spirit is proven in the battle.

Where pain and fear in Scott have an active and violent resolution, in Lampman they are resolved passively, through escape of through a slow, organic process. From the pain of the city, Lampman's poet figure commonly escapes to the comfort of the fields where, as in "The Frogs," "The voices of mankind, the outer roar, [Grow] strange and murmurous, faint and far away." It is not simply to the sensuous pleasures or the peace of the landscape he escapes, of course, but to a far more profoundly regenerative contact with universal and eternal harmonies manifested in nature. The pain is eased by a spiritual contact with nature. In "The Frogs," "Earth, our mother" allows man an intuition of "her spirit's inmost dream". The "dream" in Lampman's work, so ably explained by Roy Daniells and Sandra Djwa, is the ultimate relief for the pain suffered by the soul in the ugly and discordant world of man in the here and now.[6]

The "dream" works in a gradual healing way analogous to the organic processes of the seasons. Here is the city dweller escaped to the fields:

> As so I lie and feel the soft hours wane,
>   To wind and sun and peaceful sound laid bare,
> That aching dim discomfort of the brain
>   Fades off unseen....

Especially in his earlier work, Lampman applies the natural metaphor of the seasons to the "seasons" of man's suffering, in phrases such as "frozen fear" and "wintry grief." In "Among the Timothy" he speaks of the high poetic moods which transform his world having gone lifeless, "like those white leaves / That hang all winter, shivering dead and blind." And in "Gentleness" the movement is from "pride, self-will, and blind-voiced anger, greed, / And malice with its subtle cruelty" to gentleness, whose face is "Like April sunshine, or the summer rain." This strain of metaphor would be of only trivial interest except that it unites the ways in which the pain in nature and the pain of mankind are resolved. Each is a slow organic process as compared to the violent, cathartic resolution in Scott.

The pattern, of course, does not remain this simple. There are paradoxical elements which do not fit easily into a general view of either poet's work. In Lampman, for example, pain can result not only from the strife of man but apparently from his *striving*. As the speaker in "Among the Millet" escapes from the city, he is "Weary of hope that like a shape of stone / Sat near at hand without a smile or moan." This is reminiscent of the passage in a letter to Thomson where Lampman declares that all man's grief comes from vanity and inflated expectations.[7] Hope invites frustration. In "Peace" it is said that "Him only peace shall find / ... whose soul has set aside / Desire and hope." And more explicitly in "Even Beyond Music," the speaker rejects music as painful because it "sings only of peace and joy."

And points us here in a world of pain
To joy and all its costs

Apparently pleasure must inevitably be paid for in pain. We may see a bit of the Calvinist in Lampman here. This lyric is a late one, 1898-99, but the complete paradox of pleasure is already there in "April":

As memory of pain, all past, is peace,
And joy, dream-tasted, hath the deepest cheer.

Despite the obvious Keatsean bent of the lines, they are very characteristic Lampman. They carry the fear that the perfection of joy in the ideal realm may be sullied by being imperfectly realized in the actual, but taken with Lampman's other comments about desire and pleasure, the statement has another side. Not only can joy be a source of pain, but pain can be in some way necessary to peace. Both of these implications have a negative quality which goes beyond the passiveness of Lampman's usual escape from pain, and the negative impression grows as we look more closely at the vision of peace Lampman attains to. The townspeople in "A Vision of Twilight," for example, are wise because there the spirit has united the flesh and the sublime:

Made the eyes of men far-seeing
And their souls as pure as rain,
They declare the ends of being
And the sacred need of pain.

This belief in "the sacred need of pain," like some other features of Lampman's ideals of peace, suggests that the vision as a whole is shaped to an unusual degree by an awareness of pain, almost a fascination with pain.

If there is a corresponding paradox in Scott's poetic world it is characteristically expressed in the action of the narrative poems. The forces of nature are totally ambivalent, richly responsive to the human drama but quite indifferent to human desires. In "Night Hymns," as the hymns are sung, "All wild nature stirs with the infinite, tender / Plaint of a bygone age," yet the thunderstorm sweeps down to overwhelm the singing. The human actions in response to pain and fear have themselves a curiously constructive-destructive quality: the old woman in "The Forsaken" cuts bait from her own flesh to catch the fish; the girl in "At the Cedars" takes to the water after her love though it means certain death; Keejigo submits herself to one sort of brutal pain to escape another; the medicine chief Powassan deliberately invokes all the bitterness and hatred in his spiritual world. The paradoxical, even perverse side of human psychology both Lampman and Scott uncover is not unfamiliar to any of us, nor is it a merely incidental element, but a consistent part of their treatment of strong negative emotion.

The place Lampman assigns to the human will is also consistent with his passive response to pain and his paradoxical view of desire and hope. If the peace which succeeds pain is to be achieved only by the soul that has set aside desire, then the human will must be surrendered too. The familiar passive observer in "In November" is "a creature without wish or will." Here he could simply be adopting a Wordsworthian kind of "wise passiveness," but his very meagre response to the promise of light and warmth in the autumn scene — "a sort of spectral happiness" — suggests something more than the will held in abeyance. In the earlier nature poems, "April," "Heat," "Among the Timothy," the surrender of will seems to be a way of admitting the restorative power of nature. In "The Frogs" the "divine sweet wonder-dream" is a restorative after pain, but temporary, since the voices of manking, the outer roar, must be faced eventually. In the later poems of vision, however, the loss of will seems to become a permanent condition of the wise inhabitants of various utopias. In "The Frost Elves," for example, the souls take their eternal repose "With never the breath of desire, without will."

The role that Scott assigns to the human will provides a sharp contrast. The Indian woman in "The Forsaken" must not only catch the fish, she must face the journey, "Wolf-haunted and lonely," to the fort. But the more subtle and extreme trial of her will is in the second half of the poem, where she must overcome not outside forces, but her own stubborn nature which, for three days, refuses to die. The Métis girl in "At Gull Lake" chooses her fate and accepts its brutality: "Keejigo held her face to the fury / And made no sound." Even the old woman in "A Scene at Lake Manitou," faced with the pain of her son's death, does something about it. She throws her gramophone in the lake to appease the "Powers of the Earth" who might spare her son; she rages against the fate she knows is inevitable:

> And five men held her until,
> Not conquered by them
> But subdued by her own will
> She lay still.

Then, having done what she can, she puts up her hair, tidies her dress, and prepares to borrow a grub-stake and go back to trapping for herself. These are all native characters, but Scott generalizes the necessity for human will elsewhere, as in the comparison of the ship to the human soul quoted above, and in "Lines in Memory of William Morris," where he tells the story of Akoose as a kind of parable upon his friend's life. Akoose, blind and helpless, will not submit passively to death until he has caught a pony and ridden to the scenes of his youth in one last heroic assertion of his will. The lines which preceed the tale are for Morris:

> To the end — effort — even beyond the end.

What these restricted comparisons focus our attention upon are certain qualities of the poetic worlds of Lampman and Scott which extend beyond the poems dealing with pain and fear. Lampman's visionary world, with its denial of active will, its silver-gray beauty, its nearness to pain, is more than just austere. Its everlasting rest is haunted by shadows of death. "The Land of Pallas", for example, is first described as "a happy land where strife and care were dead" — a curiously negative way of getting at the idea of peace and contentment. The visionary land in "Inter Vias" enjoys perpetual spring, yet some of the language and imagery leaves a chilly, bloodless impression. The natural, uncultivated landscape is described as "a waste that no husbandman tills." "The blood-root kindles at dawn / Her spiritual taper of snow." This spiritualized land can be seen only by "babies," "great-hearted seer of old," and poets. The only inhabitant, "the mother immortal, its queen," is described as "a presence remote and serene," a "figure slow-moving, divine, / With inscrutable eyes." A similar air of ascetic renunciation pervades a number of other poems, and while "Inter Vias" is not one of the better-known visions, it appears to have been a favorite of Lampman's. In a letter to Thomson he calls it a "piece I very much liked when I wrote it," and says "I have rarely given so much work to anything."[8]

"A Vision of Twilight" may owe a lot to Poe, but it fits in with the dark and unearthly quality of many of Lampman's later visions. The whole first stanza is worth quoting.

> By a void and soundless river
> On the outer edge of space,

> Where the body comes not ever,
> But the absent dream hath place,
> Stands a city tall and quiet,
> And its air is sweet and dim;
> Never sound of grief or riot
> Makes it mad, or makes it grim.

Here is an explicitly idyllic place surrounded by connotations of absence, the void, dimness, grief, riot, madness and grimness. Something in the heart sinks at the prospect. With its gray water, gray skies, and gray sounds, its virtues seem entirely negative. The inhabitants are "women of a spiritual rareness," moulded by old passion and old woe. And men who have escaped the struggles of life and now "rest and dream forever" "with hearts serene and whole." They have evidently escaped pain, but the world that they inherit is deathly.

The precise way in which death shadows Lampman's visions is difficult to describe. Referring to "In November," Frye mentions "the wonderful *danse macabre* in which it closes,"⁹ and some suspicion of the macabre attends the still gray pleasures in most of Lampman's visionary worlds, especially in the later poetry. The Frost Elves describe a land which combines the macabre with Lampman's unearthly passiveness, renunciation of will, and enjoyment of a sombre, remote, and austere kind of peace. It is in "the valley of perfect repose"; the inhabitants are ghosts on the frozen battlements of the city.

> Peasants and emperors, old and young,
> They fronted the low sunrise
> They sat with no sound; and the hoar frost hung
> In the width of their passionless eyes.

They bring to mind "the City of the End of Things." These spirits, "who could never find rest upon earth," have achieved a kind of perfection by renunciation of desire and will. They had been men:

> Who lived at the uttermost tension of life
> In the power of its pitiless need,
> Whose night was of dreams and their day was of strife
> But now they have peace indeed;

Again the ghostly world seems fashioned largely by a not entirely successful attempt to escape pain and its sources as Lampman discerned them.

One of the most deathlike details of these ghostly visions of beauty and peace is the silence, and this silence appears outside the dream visions. In "Winter — Solitude," for example, the poet sees a winter landscape like a "petrified sea," with much of the pale-gray beauty of the vision poems. The poet is at peace:

> In a world so mystically fair
> So deathly silent...

What Lampman gives us is less a silence of contemplation or peace than a fascinated hovering on the edge of the ultimate silence of death.

Looking at pain and fear in Scott leads us not only toward violence and struggle in the narrative poems but toward a darkness which is more general in his poetic world. As A.J.M. Smith has pointed out, Scott was fascinated with darkness.[10] A surprising number of his poems, and most of those for which he is remembered, are either set at night or marked by prominent imagery of darkness. (How often do we remember, for example, that "Spring on Mattagami" and "The Height of Land" are both night reveries?) Pain and fear and the struggle against them often appear as a dynamic tension between images of darkness and images of light. The killers in "On the Way to the Mission" dog the Indian through the day, and when "the spruces are dark with sleep" they kill him. He falls "on a shield of moonlight." Keejigo in "At Gull Lake" is named for the light, "star of the morning," and at her destruction there is not only the darkness of storm and oncoming night, but the imagery, as she returns to her husband, of "death-black water."

In poems of struggle the balance of light is often precarious. An image from "Rapids at Night" is suggestive. Under what is described as a "great dome of darkness" there is "a little light, cast by foam under starlight." This is the setting for the "abysmal roar" of the rapids which speak with "one voice, deep with the sadness, / That dwells at the core of all things."

Where the balance is disturbed, the whole is commonly resolved into darkness. In "Night Burial in the Forest," the funeral party take away their torch and "withdraw the little light from the ocean of gloom." The darkness can be accompanied by peace, the end of the struggle with pain, the freeing of the soul. Here the murdered warrior is at rest: "He who feared nought will fear ought never," and the wind becomes the "wings of the angel who gathers the souls from the wastes of the world." Similarly, in "The Forsaken," as the old woman dies, "all light was gathered up by the hand of God and hid in his breast."

But darkness can remain identified with the forces the soul struggles against. Powassan, drumming up "hated things vanished" and "hated things to come" evokes a dark response in nature:

> And the cloud rears up
> To the throbbing of Powassan's Drum.
> An infusion of bitter darkness
> Stains the sweet water of twilight.

In "Night Hymns" the opposition between the Christian spirit and the menacing wilderness is established in light and dark imagery beginning with this first stanza:

> Here in the midnight, where the dark mainland and island
> Shadows mingle in shadow deeper, profounder,

Sing we the hymns of the churches, while the dead water
  Whispers before us.

In this deepening darkness the stars gleam in the lake from the edge of the stormcloud, then vanish. At the same time the song lives briefly at the edge of the thunder before it is drowned out. The darkness becomes more enveloping: the ripple of the canoe "Lapses in blackness," the whirlpools are carried "Down into darkness" just as the notes of the song "falter / Back into quiet." Then the storm "Whelms them in splendid hollows of booming thunder." It is a triumph of darkness, and one we are invited to glory in.

The precarious venturing of the human spirit into the essentially dark world is aptly imaged in the fragile bark canoe afloat on the lonely lake in a rising storm, and the image is appropriate to Scott's poetry. The metaphor of the spirit as a point of light flickering in the infinite darkness is extended in Scott's non-wilderness poems. In "Labour and the Angel" the old man works in the darkness of blindness; the little girl is his light, his eyes, and to the poet's mind she is the spirit which attends upon work and blesses it. The light which the couple in "The Flight" have against the storm is explicitly love.

However pervasive the darkness in Scott's poetic world, it is hard to escape a sense of bouyancy and optimism which contrasts strongly with the resignation in much of Lampman's work. First of all, there is beauty even in the violence of the storm, which transcends the human fates involved. Also, though darkness may evoke fear in the characters of the poem, in some larger view it often represents something unknown, as it does in "The Forsaken," rather than something evil. Finally, there is what might be called the reassuring tone of Scott's faith. In "Night Hymns," for example, the darkness prevails, but the most arresting feature of the scene is that the spirit continues to venture out against it. The song flies out "like a dove," a promise of peace, hope, grace. Scott offers the same affirmation in a more general way in "Meditation at Pergia," where he says:

While the last sunset smoulders in the West,
Still the great faith with the undying hope
  Upsprings and flows

In Scott's discussion of death in "Lines in Memory of William Morris," there is another solid note of faith in the life of the spirit, when he says "That something will escape of soul or essence." That "something" seems to be what contends with the darkness.

Out of the deathly silence of Lampman's vision and the darkness in Scott's there rises the question of how convincingly pain and fear have been resolved in either world. The pain especially seems to have invaded Lampman's dream in a variety of oblique ways. And all that Scott finally offers as a defence against what he calls in "The

Nightwatchman" his "dread of darkness" is an insistence upon faith, not a demonstration of how faith triumphs.

To look concertedly at the resolution of pain and fear in Lampman and Scott means, of course, to overlook a great deal of their poetry. Lampman was also a poet of ecstatic lyrics and calm descriptive verse. Scott was, as Gary Geddes says, "a piper of many tunes,"[11] but the darkness we find associated with pain and fear seems to me to dominate some of Scott's most successful and most distinctive poetry. I would also say that the shadowy areas of Lampman's poetic world which extend from his treatment of pain and fear are not far from the centre of his poetic vision.

NOTES

[1] "Lampman's Fleeting Vision", *Canadian Literature*, no. 56 (Spring 1973), 28.

[2] "Memoir of Duncan Campbell Scott", in *Selected Poems of Duncan Campbell Scott* (Toronto: Ryerson, 1951), p. xxv.

[3] "The Significance of Lampman", rpt. in *Archibald Lampman*, ed. Michael GNAROWSKI (Toronto: Ryerson, 1970), p. 189.

[4] "Duncan Campbell Scott", in *Our Living Tradition*, Second and Third Series, ed. Robert L. McDOUGALL (Toronto: University of Toronto Press, 1959), p. 77.

[5] "Duncan Campbell Scott", in his *Ten Canadian Poets* (Toronto: Ryerson, 1958), p. 164.

[6] DJWA, "Lampman's Fleeting Vision", and Roy Daniells, "Lampman and Roberts," in *Literary History of Canada*, gen. ed. Carl F. KLINCK (Toronto: University of Toronto Press, 1965), pp. 389-98.

[7] Arthur S. BOURINOT, ed., *Archibald Lampman's Letters to Edward William Thomson* (Ottawa: The Editor, 1956), p. 33.

[8] BOURINOT, p. 23.

[9] "Canada and Its Poetry", rpt. in *The Making of Modern Poetry in Canada*, ed. Louis DUDEK and Michael GNAROWSKI (Toronto: Ryerson, 1967), p. 95.

[10] SMITH, p. 78.

[11] "Piper of Many Tunes, D.C. Scott", *Canadian Literature*, no. 37 (Summer 1968), 15-27.

BARRIE DAVIES

THE FORMS OF NATURE: SOME OF THE PHILOSOPHICAL AND AESTHETIC BASES OF LAMPMAN'S NATURE POETRY

It is more difficult than one has been led to believe to find in Lampman a simple aesthetic response to natural beauty. That this is there is not disputed, and has been rightly appreciated. However, to read or condemn Lampman as a mere poet of the Ontario landscape is either impossible or unjust, for his response quickly moves from the simple to the complicated and profound. Lampman was conscious of this and dramatises in his poetry what he suggests in his theory, the possible reactions to nature.

This suggestion accounts for the various people in his poetry who have a necessary or instinctive, but not articulate relationship with the natural world. One example is the woodcutter in "The Woodcutter's Hut," others are the wagooner in "Heat," at one level Richard in "The Story of an Affinity," the woodmen and ploughmen in "In November," the little old brown woman" in "Across the Pea Fields," and so on. In "On the Companionship With Nature" (pp. 258-259) he reserves his disapproval (in a manner which recalls Wordsworth's sonnet "The world is too much with us") for those who merely exploit nature. Lampman's own description of the more meaningful relationship of the poet is important because it sets forth in simplified terms the complex aesthetic which he strove to formulate and practise in his poetry. The title of his poem is "The Poet's Possession" (p. 157) and the possession, of course, is the creative imagination.

Lampman is reminding us that the simple material response is not the only or the most significant one. It is characteristic of Lampman to interpret the poetic process in terms of natural imagery. Poetry for him was an organic process. Experience can be made to yield more than material results if approached in the right way. A "crop of images" is an apt phrase which graphically captures the poetic process of image association growing towards final synthesis. Not the least important is the implicit endorsement of the value of the poet and poetry, of the total response without which life remains unexamined. Bearing these views in mind it is not surprising that Lampman felt Emerson to be a nature poet "in the fullest sense."[1] In describing Emerson's relationship to nature, and by implication the ideal poetic relationship, he writes:

> Emerson's sympathy with nature is not however in the main that of the observer, the student or the artist; it is a sympathy of force, a cosmic sympathy. He is drawn to nature because in the energies of his own soul he is aware of a kinship to the forces of nature and feels with an elemental joy, as if it were part of himself, the eternal movement of nature.[2]

Lampman once more carefully distinguishes between the various approaches to nature. A really meaningful relationship is not established by the casual tourist, by the naturalist given to description of minutiae, or by the representational painter. These approaches are juxtaposed with the creative one of the nature poet. This is vital, compulsive and universal, because of the nature of the universe itself. The correspondence of a force within to a force without results in a breaking down of subject and object, a physical dissolution so complete that the subjective is felt to contain the infinite, or what Lampman characteristically describes as "eternal movement." This awareness brings an "elemental joy." However, it follows, and this is important if one would understand the darker moments which adumbrate other Lampman poems, that when this identity fails to manifest itself or proves incapable of being achieved, "cosmic sympathy" may be replaced by cosmic alienation. It will also be seen that the meaning of nature is vastly expanded beyond an awareness of physical forms.

The best description of his poetry is provided by himself. In his essay on Keats he writes that poetry:

> should be clear, spontaneous and inevitable as the movement of the universe itself. It should only deal with such things as in their essences should accord with that divine and universal harmony.[3]

Lampman concentrates on three aspects of poetry: form, concern, and purpose. What Lampman calls "things" are simply material objects and the "essence" is that which defines the essential nature of the object. A variety of objects, no matter how apparently disparate, may have in common a defining nature. We have moved then from a material world of diverse phenomena to an intellectual world of concepts or ideas. Lampman was familiar with Plato and his basic philosophy is ultimately Platonic. Plato's theory of ideas was a synthesis in many ways of previous Greek philosophy. It combined first of all the theory of Heraclitus, that of perpetual flux resolved in the principal element of fire; secondly, the theory of Xenophanes which stated that the universe is permeated by God, that the Many reflect the One; thirdly, the Socratic method of induction.

In Lampman's best poetry, of course, we feel that we are never being offered secondhand abstraction but always an original, characteristic, and personal poetic meaning. The aesthetic is more interesting and complex because it is the result of a many-sided response to experience as opposed to an intellectual one alone. From this point of view the "things" dealt with are usually natural objects. Poetry is "spontaneous" and "inevitable," that is, appearing instinctive and thus unavoidable. It is partly a matter of selection concerned with essence and correspondence. Consequently the poet's first task is the perception of the unique quality of an object which is accomplished through the use of the primary poetic faculty, the creative imagination. This faculty penetrates and impregnates matter with meaning. It isolates the significance of an object by enclosing its essential quality in an image. Aesthetically, the essence is the image. The continual working of the creative imagination results in a number of images from which the under-standing or conceptual part of the mind constructs a pattern. The "universal movement," or the "divine and universal harmony," is conceived of not as an abstraction, but as a symbol, of which the image is part, either in shape or quality or both. The symbol is the totality of meaning contained by the image pattern, or to use Lampman's more expressive phrase, "image crop," and something more, because the whole is greater than the sum of the parts.

Lampman's aesthetic assigns the dominant and active role to the creative imagination. The intellect controls and orders the essential perceptions. The instinct or extreme sensory awareness stimulates the creative imagination and balances the tendency of the intellect towards abstraction by providing a counterweight of passion. When the poetic process is working perfectly the three elements co-operate harmoniously and the movement is towards fusion and synthesis. But, of course, in other states or moods, there is a tendency for the intellect to usurp its function by working analytically and thus strangling the creative process. The poetic process is organic until a pattern is established and becomes finally, with a further enlargement of meaning, symbolic. The aesthetic theory may be left at this for the time being as a later discussion of Lampman's most important poems will provide clarification and permit the demonstration of palpable significance which the theory can only imply.

A final observation remains then to be made at this juncture. Lampman is a landscape poet, but in an important and special sense. It should be clear from the discussion of his aesthetic that a "landscape" very easily and quickly takes on a symbolic meaning for the poet. This is not to say that the landscape does not have its own material validity, for the symbolic approach does not remove qualities from the object, rather it enlarges the significance contained within it.

Nature, then, is instinct, with meaning for mankind, over and above the immediately evident material one. It is this belief which partly explains an aspect of Lampman's poetic method. This aspect mirrors also an important and relevant need. With these observations in mind, the discussion may begin by recalling that Lampman, because of his classical education, would have been familiar with the response of the Greeks to nature. If the universe is viewed symbolically there can be no isolation since everything is linked by correspondence and assimilation. The Greeks were aware of a world rich in meaning and this is partly why Lampman admired them. Shelley, in an attempt to define the importance of the Greek poets for himself, wrote to Peacock:

> I now understand why the Greeks were such great poets, and above all, I can account, it seems to me, for the harmony, the unity, the perfection, the uniform excellence, of all their works of art. They lived in perpetual commerce with external nature and nourished themselves upon the spirit of its forms.[4]

In "June" (p. 140) Lampman describes one aspect of his poetic method; here the "dreamers" are synonymous with poets, and in particular, the myth-making Greek poets. Lampman isolates the main "figure" or characteristic of myth-making personification.

"Among the Millet" (p. 3) is a direct statement of a mythological intuition of the natural world. The poem begins with the poet looking at the clouds. In the second stanza it is the qualities of the clouds which the poet becomes aware of as they move, merge, separate, and reform. The mythological impulse then begins and the poet recalls the "men of old" or the Greek poets. The "dream" of the fourth stanza is the myth and the easy correspondence between the natural and the supernatural is simply stated in the paradox of the final line, "the shining field of heaven." This is a straightforward poem and does not approach the resonance of Lampman's best poetry, but it does serve to illustrate Lampman's conscious symbolic approach.

If nature has values for mankind, and this is one implication of Lampman's aesthetic, then contemporary man either ignores them or is unable to respond to them. The "men of old" stand out in sharp contrast to the men of Lampman's time. The poet is placed in the painful situation of having to rationalize his own subscription to the values of nature in face of the indifference, ignorance, or incapacity of the majority. His alienation from society is made bearable by his identity through nature with a sense of universal wholeness. But such identity is only won through constant struggle and is not always obtainable. The poems of struggle are often Lampman's most interesting ones and are the guarantors of his sincerity. They put paid to objections that Lampman's affinity with nature was over-easy or merely factitious.

Lampman implies that ideally men may identify themselves with the values of nature. That they are unable to, or do not wish to, within the present culture makes Lampman, in the less obviously social poems, re-interpret the theological implications of the Fall in terms of the defective or stunted sensibilities of mankind and a resulting "culture" which is a perversion of the primary meaning of the word. To put it another way, nature maintains organic values. If this is recognised then the simplest material detail is capable of infinite expansion and infinite correlation. The practical effect of such recognition is to humanise inasmuch as it exercises a total response. But if the organic principle is not perceived, then it is distorted into its malevolent counterpart and encourages the atrophy of all that is most characteristically human. The end, as Lampman so clearly shows us, is inessential "things."

Men continue to live in unwisdom because of a lost capacity to see, as Emerson said, the miraculous in the commonplace, and nature is commonplace in the sense that it may be taken for granted and therefore never "seen." Even when it is noticed, the response is partial and superficial because men's senses have been dulled. Lampman's sonnet "Sight" (p. 111) is therefore Biblical in its injunction. Clearly the senses are important, but,

> We are comparatively deaf and dumb and blind, and without smell or taste or feeling.... the ears were made not for such trivial uses as men are wont to suppose, but to hear celestial sounds. The eyes were not made for such grovelling uses as they are now put to and worn out by, but to behold beauty now invisible.... What is it then to educate, but to develop these divine germs called the senses?[5]

In "Winter Store" (pp. 165-173) Lampman endorses Thoreau's words. Because Lampman is trying to say too much in it, the poem is not a complete success, and only at times does it enjoy a rich, complex compression. The poet appeals to men to be "subtly conscious," that is, to know and feel in a finely discerning and acute way. If the senses can be cultivated to such an extent that "the whole body is one sense, and imbibes delight through every pore," then as Lampman says, the forms of nature become "emblems of pure pleasures" which is the starting point for apprehensions still finer. Man is a "chrysalis." He remains undeveloped and ugly. His state is significantly located in images derived from the sordid aspects of the modern city; "the narrow alley," and the verbs of movement, "plod" and "creeping" emphasize the heavy, the dull, and the undignified low level of sentient being. Because the senses are dulled, the moral, spiritual and intellectual being remains unengaged.

The second stanza evokes the miracle of the ordinary through the use of paradox and apt metaphor. What is caught here is the expansion of the original perception; a minute becomes an hour, and the hour leads to time itself. The metaphor of time as a rainbow and a gate is complex. The rainbow combines the symbols of light and water. The fertility associations of rain are illuminated. Furthermore, as an arc or incomplete circle, the rainbow suggests the circle of eternity. Time is thus a part of eternity and a gateway to eternity. The final, apprehension of the poet, as opposed to the poem, is not, however, joyous and affirmative, but tragic. The poet wishes to convince himself that his vision will serve him as a talisman, "when the darker days shall come" and I think we are compelled to read this as meaning something more than merely winter. But the vision is blotted out by a more powerful and oppressive one "of the labouring world." There follows an agonised, compulsive return to contemporary civilization inimical in its fragmentation to the perception of cultural, organic, and universal wholeness. The poem ends with a fading of the image of harmony, of the men of Greece who recall the figures on Keats' urn. Thus it is tragic in a personal sense. For the reader of the poem, the effect is similar to the cathartic experience ascribed to Greek tragedy, inasmuch as the organic vision balances and resolves the opening statement. The simplicity of these final lines should not be allowed to disarm our perception of their quality. They are woven through with the close interrelationship of man with nature. The circular images of harmony are pervasive, "wreathed," capturing the correspondence of man and nature and also the "line" always on the point of becoming a circle.

One of the themes inherent in the final part of the poem can be conveniently clarified at this point. The idea that contemporary culture threatens and only permits the poet to maintain the organic vision temporarily is present in a much better poem, "Winter Evening" (p. 243). The idea is now worked out within the actual context of contemporary civilization; the two elements of its title, winter and evening, taking on a symbolic resonance, only partially realised in the loosely diffused "Winter Store." Desmond Pacey describes the octave as 'optimistic,'[6] but the word is not really appropriate to the tragic inevitability which is present there. After all, the season is winter and the time is evening, and the knowledge that night is oppressively near is not evaded. Moreover, verbs and images of uniformity, constriction and death, "whitened," "narrow," "rows," "crowded chimneys," "die" are emphatically present. Finally from the point of view of structure alone, Lampman is careful not to complete the octave without the half line, "Soon, soon, shall fly." It is important to notice that there is no suggestion of something passing, of change or renewal; sound has been replaced by silence and all movement is "still." The final realisation is of a universe that is cold, dark and petrified.

In the present discussion a central poem is "The Frogs." (p. 7) Men's senses in their degenerate state are adequate only for coping with mundane reality. In "The Frogs" Lampman explores the need, or rather the compulsion, of certain men to push beyond the generally accepted, the limits often imposed by men upon themselves. There is a sense in which Lampman is a voyageur of the imagination engaged in lonely exploration of that region of disparity between the actual and the ideal, of appearance and reality. Characteristically, and in this case logically, he locates his theme not in the sublime and imposing aspects of nature but in those insignificant and unregarded creatures, frogs. Once more Lampman is saying that the apparently insignificant is in reality pregnant with meaning, if correctly apprehended.

The first stanza realises a Platonic order underlying the world of transience and flux. The frogs are simultaneously the instinctive and articulate extension of an organic order. Their knowledge is significantly "won without a quest," and they serve as mediators between man and nature. Lampman's obligation, previously touched upon to account for man's present degenerate state, explains the time shift in the second stanza. The frogs have been made nature's functionaries because of the need to communicate to mankind her "dream," that is the steadfast and eternal order, "ever at rest beneath life's change and stir."

There follows an evocation of the creation of this "dream" in terms which recall the rythms and detail of Genesis. With the exception of man, the creation is complete, though uninformed by purpose. As yet,

> earth the mother dreamed with brooding brow,
> Musing on life and what the hours might be.

The fixed creative principle of the universe is love and the creation becomes purposive only when "love should ripen into maternity." Love can contain maternity, but maternity is only an aspect of love. Maternity, in other words, is nature, the essence of which is fertility. Love is the active will to create, to impregnate matter with meaning, which is why nature is meaningful. Though the principle of creation is fixed, it incorporates the seeds of movement or growth towards maternity which is a more dynamic aspect of love.

The voices of the frogs, then, express the informed purpose of nature, and as they sing the movement of life begins, "the great buds swelled." The fifth stanza returns in time to the present in which the poet's apparent alienation appears logically motivated and reasonable. The description of "the outer roar," or the voices of mankind opposed to those of the frogs, as "strange" is felt to be exact when we realise that it is the society of men which is in fact alien to an order of which the poet is a part. In the last four lines there is a willing return to the world of flux, a return which is not this time accompanied by pain and loss. Here the poet's insight sustains him; that is, the dream remains the reality, and so-called "reality," though recognised, is not felt to be oppressive.

Together with the poet and the "men of old" there is a final group of individuals which should be discussed. The discussion of this group will also provide the starting point for a scrunity of a further preoccupation of Lampman, the nature of the poetic process itself.

With important reservations, Lampman would have endorsed Thoreau's view that:

> Fishermen, hunters, woodchoppers, and others spending their lives in the woods, in a peculiar sense a part of nature themselves, are often in a more favourable mood for observing her, in the intervals of their pursuits, than philosophers or poets even....[7]

What these men have in common in the essentially lonely and vagrant nature of their calling. Likewise the poet is an isolated itinerant in the realm of mind and spirit, but the major difference, at once the source of his difficulties and the solution of them, is the commitment to articulateness. The poem, "The Woodcutter's Hut," is one in which both the instinctive and articulate relationships with nature are present. This is one of several poems illustrating an inquiry into the physical and mental state most favourable to the appreciation of nature's meaning. These poems, though marked by struggle, are characterised by integrity and are in essence affirmative, for the very human reason that Lampman is at work in his characteristic activity. They stand in marked contrast to those stark poems such as "Midnight," which are a record of what Lampman elsewhere described as the "tragic sense of isolation" from family, society, nature, and the universe.

"The Woodcutter's Hut" (pp. 247-250) may be read on three interrelated levels. The first is necessarily the most subjective as it is concerned with the nature of the poetic process. The second can be described as anthropological, as it explores the nature of man. The third may be called cultural, since it deals with the quality of man's existence. These three levels correspond to the four "objects" in the poem, the poet, the woodcutter, the hut, and poetry itself.

The poem opens with an evocation of the wilderness in winter in which every detail is carefully selected, accreting emotional and symbolical potential as the movement unfolds. An additional dimension is provided by the hills which, as many poems reveal, have at least Biblical significance for Lampman, but the emphasis is significantly placed upon a formless landscape without colour, sound, motion, or property.

Within this landscape, the hut has almost lost its definition, being but

> a few rough
> beams that show
> A blunted peak and a low black line, from the glittering waste of snow.

Nevertheless its potential shape is not lost. The black base of the triangle, is firmly present and, though the apex or peak is "blunted", it is completed by the smoke. I will state my reading of the passage in the belief that a continuing analysis will provide sufficient evidence to warrant it. The base is substantial because the instinctive life will survive despite its apparent precariousness, but the peak is blunted because the intellectual and spiritual qualities in the woodcutter or representative man are not fully developed. It is for the same reason that the "smoke" is "thin" and "leisurely." However, the smoke does have colour, "pink," but it is pale and potential, though aspiring to Lampman's ideal form as it "curls". Furthermore, it denotes the primary element fire, and the force heat. The physical life, though circumscribed, "narrow trail," is the most aggressive and complete, asserting itself in noise. The "breath" of the woodcutter is "rythmic" and his tool, the axe, "shouts," "echoes," and "rings," capturing both sound and solid form.

In the eight lines which follow, the physical life is developed through bird, animal, and man, reaching a climax in the arrival of horses and teams. After the first climax, the opening stress is resumed and deepened with a time-shift from morning to night. The hut is besieged by the storm and the woodcutter sits before a "sinking," "wavering," "guttering," fire performing mechanical tests. Physical life now sinks to its lowest ebb, and the woodcutter is almost a hibernating animal "without thought" or memory, hardly hearing, almost unconscious, nearly pure instinct. It is at the height of the storm that the second movement of the poem ends with a promise of renewal in the vision followed by the reality of spring. There is a time-shift once more, a seasonal ont to spring and summer. The plenitude of life is vividly rendered through a piling up of sensuous detail. The forest "glimmers" not "glitters" with the warmest and most meaningful colour — "living gold." There is simultaneous noise and movement in the verbs "chime," "gusting," "prick," "lift," "uncurl," and "exalt." At the same time there are other important changes. The woodcutter becomes a farmer. He exchanges the hills for the valley, winter for summer, isolation for society, and this third section of the poem ends with an appreciation of the wholesomeness of the physical, instinctive life:

> The animal man in his warmth and vigour,
> sound and hard and complete.

However, the major key of joyous affirmation should not obscure the minor one of loss which complicates the emotional response and provides the link with the fourth section in which it is fully developed. Lampman typically breaks off his line so that the second half may lead us into the contrast:

> The sparrow shall see and exult; but lo! as the
> spring draws gaily on,
> The woodcutter's hut is empty and bare, and the
> master that made it is gone.

The woodcutter is referred to as "master," which recalls the poet's description of himself in "Winter Evening," and we are generally prepared for the shift of focus from the woodcutter to the hut, and of the position of the poet from the background to the fore. The final section of the poem brings to mind "The Poet's Possession" where after the farmer comes the poet. Here the exact opposite of the opening statement receives attention. In the midst of the winter wilderness the hut was not felt to be desolate because it contained life and had form, but as images of fertility and growth crowd upon each other they intensify the loss of form and emphasise the decay. It is left to the solitary poet, far from the society of men, to descry and articulate the meaning of the hut, to inhabit imaginatively the object and make it a symbol which gives shape and definition to the inchoate experience of mankind.

The woodcutter, then, is primarily instinctive and primitive man. He is associated with the basic necessities of life, wood for fuel and warmth, shelter, tools to be used in agriculture for the production of food. However, he is also, at the crudest level, man as maker. The wood he cuts not only provides fuel but is also worked into material for construction. The resulting form is nevertheless simply an extension of a basic need and completely functional.

The woodcutter's contribution is at the rudimentary level of construction, of which the highest expression and the most complete is the arts and literature followed by craftsmanship. The woodcutter's creation is without aesthetic value and is fragile and impermanent. Nevertheless it does have qualities which are important for the poet. In a forest it is made from wood. In its simplicity it eschews the superfluous and exactly reflects a need. Though the work of man it blends closely and easily with nature in all seasons. On the one hand, then, we have the woodcutter, instinctive man with his rudimentary construction; on the other, the poet, configurative man, and his expression, which is capable of giving mankind a much fuller sense of itself.

This may be put in another way in order to clarify another side of the same theme. The woodcutter represents a strong instinctive faculty whilst the poet is primarily creative imagination together with reason and instinct. The instinct is not to be underrated or devalued, for without it there can be no life of any kind and its withdrawal means death. The poetic process depends upon a careful balance of the three faculties. Though a poem can never be the result of instinct alone, it should appear to have in its total qualities some which closely resemble instinct. When Lampman stated that poetry should be "spontaneous" and "inevitable" he stated two of these qualities and symbolised the ideal synthesis in the frogs. In other words, poetry should resemble nature as closely as possible, and this result is best achieved when art conceals art.

Lampman's long narrative poem "The Story of an Affinity" (pp. 411-473) provides a convenient link between the present discussion and a closer scrutiny of a number of poems which deal specifically with the constituents of the poetic character and the problems which it confronts. "The Story of an Affinity" is a significant poem because it manages to incorporate many of Lampman's most personal themes. The neglect and obscurity into which it has fallen is the probable result of a conventional and dated structure. A closer inspection, however, reveals the poem's central importance.

The protagonist of the poem, Richard, a farmer's son, appears to be an intelligent child who his father hopes will benefit from education and become a professional man. But as the child becomes older, his intellectual promise seems to wither and die whilst he grows physically imposing. For the most part, with his eyes either staring fixedly or completely

84

blank, he seems stupid. Occasionally he is possessed by a "force" which drives him to perform feats of manual labour or to wander restlessly about the countryside. Richard is man in the process of becoming. His environment:

> The monotonous life
> of those whose only care is with the earth

permits the growth of the physical, but discourages the growth of the intellectual and spiritual. It is true the farmer has contact with nature, but, as we have seen, he has only a partial and material one, the employment of "unloved forces" which produces an insensitive attitude to nature. In order to understand what takes place from this point onwards Lampman's description of Emerson, already quoted, should be kept in mind. Richard is not merely one of the "pale multitude," but possesses what Lampman calls in his essay "Happiness," "energy of life" which is the source of his present difficulties and future achievements. The energy is present but is "smouldering," "fitful," "ungoverned," "lawless," "blind," "witless" and amoral. Richard's sensibilities, like those of most around him, are unawakened and he is indifferent to the natural world.

It takes a more extreme manifestation of the energy of nature to release him from the narrow prison of the self, the noise of the roaring wind, "the sound and moving majesty of wind and wood". The wind is the expression of nature's force most akin to that which possesses Richard, and a momentary sympathy is established. Richard moves from the instinctive to the aware. This temporary awareness of kinship provokes an immediate need, extreme and anguished, for expression, caught in Lampman's description of the physical contortion of Richard's limbs and features.

He is incapable of the "tremendous word" or poetry and thus finds relief in ripping up a young birch tree, a response to a complex experience that is partial, simple, and ultimately unsatisfactory. His awareness becomes permanent when he encounters the beauty of Margaret which more importantly provides him with a glimpse of a further extension of perception, the creative principle of the universe, love. The "power unlocked," however, brings both joy and terror. The awareness brings joy, but also fear when awareness illuminates the sorry quality of Richard's life to that moment and his incapacities. However, Margaret's book becomes a symbol, and the conch-shell which calls the farm hands for food calls Richard to feed his mind as well as his body.

It is now possible to make a general comment which will draw together and summarise the somewhat scattered observations arising from the discussion of inndividual poems, and serve also as an introduction to an examination of the intellectual correspondence of nature.

The constant patterning of Lampman's nature poetry was not

achieved accidentally. Such order was felt to have an objective existence and was simultaneously a characteristic of the poet's shaping vision. As a co-relationist Lampman saw in nature and embodied in his poetry the quaternary principle. Most obviously, as even a superficial look at his poetry reveals, he was preoccupied with the movement of the seasons. The onset of winter was felt with the same emotional intensity that the death and resurrection of Christ would have for the orthodox Christian. The four seasons, Spring, Summer, Autumn, and Winter have their counterparts in a diurnal pattern. Spring is associated with dawn or the morning, Summer with noon, Autumn with afternoon, and Winter with evening or night. Furthermore, there is a realtionship with the four points of the compass and the four elements. Thus Spring is associated with the East and air; Summer with the South and fire; Autumn with the West and water; and Winter with the North and earth.

But the topography of Lampman's "universe" includes much more than the physical or naturalistic. It accounts for, first of all, the stages of personal existence and periods of human history. The Spring is infancy, Summer is youth, Autumn is middle age and Winter is old age. In terms of human history Lampman envisaged a Golden Age which he associated with the era of the Greeks, or, as his poem "To Chaucer" (pp. 270-271) shows, with the Middle Ages. There are also in his essay on Keats some revealing remarks. The early Romantic period represented a golden age typically evoked in fresh Classical and natural imagery. His own age was felt to be one of solitude and self-reflection in which the poet consolidated and maintained the perceptions and culture of previous ages in face of indifference and encroaching hostility to artistic endeavours and values.

It is appropriate that my discussion of the meaning of the external forms of nature has led me to the verge of intellectual, moral, and artistic concerns. It is only by making artificial distinctions that these levels of meaning can be discussed individually, for the experience of reading the poetry is to encounter them in their total and interacting complexity. The celebration of physical nature, including the physical nature of man, is but partial and insufficient. Nature engages the intellectual and spiritual faculties of the poet. The poet is compelled to illuminate external nature with what he called "the conscious mind". As will be seen, this compulsive bringing of "the conscious mind" to external nature has its rewards, but it also has its difficulties and frustrations. The counterpart of the physical creation for the poet is, of course, the poem. Consequently, Lampman's ballad of life is most importantly concerned with the nature of artistic endeavour. His response to the external forms of nature was acutely sensitive, but this was a prelude to a more complicated response when:

> the forms of unseen things present themselves to our imaginations with a vividness and reality of detail rarely at other times attained. Out on a country road, walking in a silent and quiet downfall of snow, when distances are veiled and hidden, and my mind seems wrapped about and softly thrown in upon itself by a smooth and caressing influence, I become immersed in the same depth and intensity of reflection.[8]

Here we have an example of the poet's typical creative stance, a blotting out of external detail and a moving inwards to subjective configuration. The experience is akin to that described by Wordsworth in "Tintern Abbey" where the "life of things" is very close to Lampman's "essence." However, the creative and receptive state is rare and infrequent, and it is time now to look at a number of important poems which express what most impedes the free working of the creative imagination.

An earlier quotation from Thoreau should be recalled and completed. Those men who live close to nature, such as woodcutters, fishermen and hunters, and partake of the instinctive life, are often in a "more favourable mood" for observation of nature compared with philosophers and poets "who approach her with expectation." The key word here is "expectation." The poet has a compulsive need to order and rationalise the world of phenomena. But this very striving after order is a forcing, an intellectualising of the creative process which in itself, as we have seen, must closely resemble the spontaneous and inevitable workings of nature. Such an attitude is unfavourable to creation and is accompanied not by a synthesis of perception but by analytical disintegration and abstraction.

In "An Old Lesson From The Fields" (p. 111), the poet is rapt in the contemplation of the movement and sounds of nature. He understands that he is observing an unconscious and continuous process of perpetual becoming. His understanding moves to an affinity of experience, and momentary identification leads to an objectivity which critically reflects his ordinary existence:

> And saw myself made clear as in a glass,
> How that my soul was for the most part dead.

The apostrophe to the "tall lilies of the wind-vexed field" makes clear that the concluding portion of the poem is a re-interpretation in the poet's terms of the Biblical injunction to consider the lilies of the field. In other words, "the conscious stress" of life is an enemy of life itself and art.

"To The Cricket" (p. 193) is a statement of the need to give expression to the meaning of nature. But the conscious desire, what Keats called that "irritable reaching after fact and reason," defeats its own purpose. In such a state the sounds of the cricket bring no delight but only "fret." This unpoductive state is contrasted with the necessary prelude to a favourable creative state; the willingness to be "in doubts and perplexities" or, as Lampman puts it, the capacity "to let it go," to achieve a sympathetic and instinctive affinity.

"Cloud Break" (pp. 145-146), as the title indicates, is a poem concerned with the momentary illumination of the creative imagination and the density of perception accompanying such moments. In the "infinite shrouds" of the rolling clouds which obscure the sunlight there occurs a break. The landscape is flooded with light which gives it an intensity it did not formerly possess. The meadows become a pristine green, the scents of nature are almost palpable, and the islands are ignited in a burst of varied colours. The concentration of the moment is caught in the verb "distils." The final stanza records the return of coldness and darkness to the landscape and the poetic mind.

"Winter Hues Recalled" (pp. 27-30) is a more thoroughgoing exploration of the poetic faculties in a manner which reminds one of passages of "The Prelude." The opening emphasis is placed upon images of freedom, but a kind of freedom in opposition to social restraint. The poet is concerned with what Wordsworth called "spots of time," those concentrated moments of intensity in diversity described in "Cloud Break." Multifarious activities and phenomena are noted and stored in the unconsciousness and apparently forgotten. On certain occasions, however, these provide the stuff upon which the creative imagination works. The process is continuous beneath the surface flux of mundane existence. Again we encounter the typical creative stance, the moment of "wise passiveness" when

> the heart is most at rest
> and least expectant.

The creative moment cannot be legislated into existence by intellectual need. It is akin to the natural process. It is a "garner house" whose contents "like sealed wine" need age to mellow. In such moments when the creative imagination is at work memories emerge from the unconsciousness with a startling and palpable reality.

What follows is a demonstration of the creative imagination at work; memories are ordered, selected and sifted so that essential meaning shapes experience into coherence. The poet engaged in the intense physical activity of climbing on snow shoes is "clear eyed, but unobservant." Tired, he rests on a fence and it is at this moment that the beauty of the natural scene overwhelms him. The strenuous activity has exercised and subdued his physical presence, releasing the poetic faculties. The poem, however, ends on an ambiguous note, reasserting the poet's continual emphasis upon balance. Rapt and "spell bound" in the contemplation of beauty, the poet does not feel one quality of the landscape which nevertheless exists and is dangerous to ignore, "the keen wind and deadly air." A life of contemplation has its dangers if it leads to the avoidance of material reality. Poetry and the poet cannot dispense with the possible limitations of the instinct and the passions but must serve them whilst controlling them.

"Among the Timothy" (p. 13) deals with similar themes, but in a manner which is more consciously mythological and historical. In this way, the theme becomes more inclusive, shifting back and forth amongst the primordial, the contemporary, and the personal. The poem begins with a re-creation of a vision of pre-lapsarian innocence in the by now familiar Lampman manner. It is early morning and the "beaded dew" remains. Into this pristine world is suddenly introduced the "mower," a common symbol of death, and there follows a total destruction of the natural order. I would not agree with Desmond Pacey that the wheel symbol here has "a positive fulfilling significance"[9] but rather argue that it is closer to the same symbol representing what he has described as "meaningless routine or terrifying futility." The circle is man-made, "clean" suggesting unnatural conformity, and "gray" linking with the description of "the blind, gray streets" of the city in the second stanza. The circle image, then, would seem to stand for a mechanical universe devoid of the principle of creative nature and love.

The poem now moves from Biblical myth to a dramatisation of the poet's personal situation. A sense of both historical and personal time is carefully, though unobtrusively, emphasized. There is a continuity of time, but the vision of innocence took place "long hours ago." It is now significantly noon. For the poet it is still "sweet to lie" even in the gray circle of death, for nature and man are not totally corrupted, and the poet must accept the limitations of an existence characterised by mortality.

The first stanza concludes with the first suggestion of the opposition between the intellectual and the intuitive apprehension. The poet is attempting to capture the state in which he is content not "to think but only dream." He seeks in nature to replace the murderous dissection of "the meddling intellect." The second stanza is crowded with images of the city with its noise and petty confusion, its sterile repression of hope, now "a shape of stone", and its apathy to the values of poetry or "song." At noon, the contemporary era, he seeks to remain true to the vision of the "dawning," of the Greek poets and the English Romantics. In the third stanza the effects of contemporary civilization upon the poetic temperament are evoked in natural images. The reaper has come to the poet, and as man-made civilization desecrates the landscape — so it stifles creativity. The poetic impulse is compared to an opening flower unfolding into a beautiful world of poetry, and poetic form or "rhyme" is an ever-changing, but inspiriting and ordering force like the movement of the wind. But the poetic impulse is dead now:

> like those white leaves
> That hang all winter, shivering dead and blind.

and the wind "vainly calls and grieves." The fourth stanza develops the condemnation of intellectual abstraction which has brought the poet to confusion, loss, and uncertainty before:

The crossing pathways of unbourned thought.

He attempts to "let it go," to give up "expectation" and "the conscious stress," and to move closer to spontaneity. Thus the poem moves toward the form and emotional colouring implicit in

> An ant slow-burrowing in the earthly gloom
> A spider bathing in the dew at morn.

Following on this state, the wind re-appears, but the healing process of his injured sensibilities is far from complete and the daisies recall images of innocence in corruption. The circular form of the daisies and the very name itself suggests the "distressed" eyes of "children in a crowd." Likewise the sixth stanza contains a reference to danger, the "prowling beast," whose temporary absence permits the "maenads" to emerge cautiously from their "hidden covert." Such images are absent by the eighth stanza where the recovery is felt to be complete. There is a definite primitivism here. The poet lies on the earth like a naked patient undergoing surgery. The nudity, probably metaphorical, represents a removal of contemporary conventions and compromises and a return to natural innocence. His mind is moulded and "fashioned" by the forces of nature and he is brought to a state in which he can feel and hear and "with quiet eyes behold." He now begins to participate in the paean of nature to life begun by the crickets and cicadas of the seventh stanza, and the poem climaxes in a powerful chant to, and complete identification with, the assertive and eternal life force symbolized by "the ever-journeying sun."

The final effect is achieved by a splendid confusion, or complete breakdown, between subject and object, the circumscribed life of man and time itself, sunlight, shadow, man's life-blood, and the forms of nature. There is resolution in "soaked" which completes the circle begun in "athirst" of the first stanza. The sun, the life force which has slaked its thirst in nature, returns to nature, and to the poet, life itself.

The discussion of the poetic process may be completed by an examination of four poems which together form an expressive and resourceful statement of Lampman's aesthetic. The poems are "Midnight," "Snow," "In November," and "Heat." As their titles indicate, the poems achieve the expression of differing modes of Lampman's perception. "Midnight" and "Snow" evoke a state of non-perception. "In November," with its title derived from a transitional month, illuminates a half-perception, and "Heat" is the culmination of the glory of complete perception

As its title suggests "Snow" (pp. 162-164) is the exact opposite of the process described in "Heat." Recalling the quaternary principle it is winter, the north, old-age, the approach of night. It is the withdrawal of the life-force, the absence of the sun, a world without light or heat, a body bereft of the quickening warmth, and a mind without illumination. It is petrifaction. What the poem records is the "movement" towards non-being, and away from becoming, externally and internally, objectively and subjectively. The "landscape" is the poet.

90

The poem begins in the typical paradoxical manner of Lampman. It is important to notice that the poem reproduces almost exactly the topography of "Heat" with a similar positioning of the poet and the objects of the landscape, but the poet concentrates on the significant differences. We are given first an panoramic view, but one which is rapidly diminishing. Here, in other words, the moving inwards is not felt to be voluntary as it is in "Heat"; moreover it is accompanied by a sense of threatening force and menace. "White" begins the poem and is emphasized by its position at the end of the first line. It is the paradox of "white" which the poet dwells on, at once the source of all colours, and no colour at all. In the second line, the feeling of contradiction is forcefully present in the juxtaposition of "fading" with "grow." This is the final "growth" of death. Movement ceases in the third line as the "wind dies." Visual limitation and increasing oppression is caught in 'denser" and this perception is intensified in the fourth line, "A gathering weight on roof and tree," which indicates an oppression in the world of man, "roof," and of nature, "tree". The final line reiterates the loss of objective sound and the subjective sense of hearing and suggests a sinister meaning, more fully present later in the poem, that this "fall" is noiseless and unresisted.

In the second stanza, there is increasing restriction of space and a concentration upon loss of contour and form. The idea of death and of something familiar and natural which has become unfamiliar and frightening is there in the "naked trees," which "loom spectrally," whilst the "dim white sky" appears indifferent and pitiless.

In the third stanza, the element of water, of life-giving movement and sound, is first introduced, but the streams are described as "far-sheeted" with the overtones once more of whiteness and extensive death as they "lie without a sound."

In the final stanza, the passing of time is mentioned; "the evening deepens" and the fact of death becomes explicit with "shrouded." The poet compares himself to the stream which is without movement and hidden. The stream still exists but is "buried." The hostility of external circumstances has brought inarticulateness. The external "world" is distinguished from the "dream," which is the creative imagination, and the poet is "secret" like the stream but still capable of movement, albeit clumsy and heavy as "plod" suggests. The creative capacity is not destroyed by seriously impeded; it remains in abeyance.

"Midnight" (p.34) is a very similar poem, but one which explores more closely the feeling of cosmic isolation accompanying the stifling of the creative capacities. The poem is unrelievedly stark as if language and form have been stripped to the minimum to convey the deprivation. The poet sitting in his room looks out and sees a lunar world, colourless, cold, and cruel. In the third line, "bars" suggest the developing mood of imprisonment and constriction. The external world is almost annihilated and within the room itself the fire is almost extinguished. This negation is further extended in the third stanza to include the poet himself. He hears a sound and struggles to listen and understand its meaning. We are not told explicitly what the sound is, but what it is not is appropriately realised through a series of negatives which in effect wipe out the world of man, animals, and nature. What the "crying" in the dark represents we realise if we recall a similar voice crying in the wilderness. Also useful here is a little poem, really a closely-woven extended metaphor, called "Loneliness."[10] The personality becomes a house to the outer rooms of which friends are admitted. But deep within the house is an "iron cell," the prison of the individual self. The crying voice in "Midnight" is in fact the creative spirit buried once more deep within the self.

"In November" (pp. 158-160) is more narrative and allegorical in approach than the previous poems and moves leisurely, in keeping with the mood evoked. The typical creative stance is here, the "loitering step" and "quiet eye," the purposive wandering. The clearing in the woods is characterised by "bleak." It is a place of destruction and death. The comparison of the dead mulleins to some "spare company of hermit folk" is literary, but nevertheless appropriate inasmuch as it defines the poet's personal situation. He too is a man apart and dedicated to an unworldly ideal. We are thus prepared for the empathetic identification which follows. Standing among the mulleins he becomes, because he has already much in common, "one of their company." The self is eradicated, the body is without "wish or will" and at the moment of dissolution of subject and object a gleam of sunlight "illuminates" the scene. But the qualities of the light are the same as those of the mulleins, "thin, sere," and "melancholy bright." Moreover the light is like a "half-reflected gleam." If light is reflected then the source is difficult to locate. It is not direct. Here it is even more obscure because it is only half-reflected and momentary. The perception is merely the "shadow" of constant, direct and steady illumination, and the meaning of the landscape, of nature, is only partially and temporarily understood and expressed as a "semblance," as something "spectral." Likewise the poetic imagination is working only with difficulty in a kind of limbo "betwixt cold and heat," between the complete absence of perception in "Snow" and the total comprehension and expressiveness in "Heat." The final state is paradoxical and unresolved. There is no final synthesis, "pleasure" being offset by "austere."

Coming to "Heat" (pp. 12-13) in this way is an interesting experience. It is appropriate and satisying that a Canadian poet should concentrate on Heraclitean fire as the primary element of the four. For climatic reasons and their effect upon the nature and quality of life such a choice was obviously not academic. The element is fire, the force is heat accompanied by light, and the source and form is the sun. Throughout Lampman's poetry, the sun was an extensive symbol, rich in association and meaning. This is not the place to discuss the classical associations, but elsewhere the sun is linked with Apollo, the god of light, fertility, truth and poetry, and Prometheus, the benevolent bringer of fire to mankind and source of the inventive and civilising arts. The sun is furthermore what we would now call the libido, the life force, and the sexual urge. The important property of heat is to decompose and melt matter and thus we have in the poem not so much a balance of opposites as a breaking down of the distinctions. Heat is a synthesizing force and a study of the imagery of Lampman's poetry reveals that he was familiar with the work and terminology of the alchemists, who were concerned with the transmutation of one substance into another, base metal into gold. Light means illumination and is associated with ardour and intensity. Cold, as we saw in "Snow," is the negation of heat and associated with petrification. All this is to say that there is a vast wealth of meaning underlying the poem, the energising of which on Lampman's part gives resonance without distorting or forcing the objective "reality" of the landscape. The symbol embraces both the primitive demiurge associated with sun worship and fertility rites and the Classical and Christian heritage of Western culture. It is also personal, local, and contemporary in its illustration of the perception and the process of perception, the dream realised, an aesthetic given action and form.

The form of the poem is centripetal, that is, moving from the external world to the shaping imagination which establishes the "essences" of "things" and their relationships to a larger order. The poem moves first around the poet and then within the mind of the poet. In the first line, the essential defining quality of the plains is isolated, they "reel." That is they appear to move in a special way and in a significant direction, "southward." But distance diminishes clarity, and there is a dwindling of light or loss of understanding and perception. In the second line we encounter the typical stance of the poet, a still centre in the midst of an animated landscape. The road "runs by" the poet. There is now a suggestion of other qualities of "heat," in the adjectives "white" and "bare," that become more explicit later in the poem. The Promethean element may also be destructive in excess, or if out of control, or if unwisely used. But here there is order and control, and the image of bleaching bones reminds us not only that heat is associated with the desert but also that the desert in the Bible, for example, was a place of divine revelation. It is the place opposed to fleshly concerns where the emphasis is placed on the ascetic, the spiritual, and the cleansing of worldly desires. The road not only "runs" but "swims," evoking a different form of movement in another environment. Eventually movement is dissolved and transmuted, for the road "melts" into the "glare." The physical liquefies and vanishes into light and heat. Something apparently "real" literally returns to its original source.

The poet focusses his attention next on the artifacts of man and man himself. The movement of the cart and waggoner is upward, "halfway" or "nearer" the "summit." A familiarity with Lampman's poetry reveals the symbolical significance of the position and movement and also of the kind of life which the waggoner stands for as the woodcutter, the instinctive, moves upward. The wagon moves dustily because it moves in a place of petrifaction, and its very form, slowly and with difficulty, with "idly clacking wheels," seems to be attempting to merge with the essential and universal form. One senses strongly that Lampman is making a philosophical statement on the nature of man, and evidence can be marshalled beyond what has already been provided to reinforce this intuition. The waggoner, "slouching slowly at his ease" is in the diminished state of sensual receptivity so often described by Lampman. At the same time he is "half-hidden" by the "white dust" (and the colour is significant). In "The Poets" (pp. 113-114) Lampman dwells on the medieval duality of man which persisted until the eighteenth century in Swift's *animal rationis capax*. Man like Pan is "half god, half brute" and it is the lower half of the body which is closest to the animal It is the lower half of the animal which is partially concealed in the white dust. At the same time the emphasis is placed on partial concealment. Lampman's "optimism" was for the most part careful and balanced. If then we accept that the road is transmuted, which it undeniably is, we must accept the waggoner as involved in the same process, though still on the road.

The wagon, says the poet, is the "sole thing that seems to move," and once more we are impressed by the precision of the wording. For in fact there is a great deal of violent movement in the poem contained in "reel," "swim," "flood," "burning," "spin" and "drenched," all placed in an overall context of apparent stillness. The qualitative description in the final line of stanza two, "the heat held land," is important, I submit, because it is the same kind of meaning as the topography of Eliot's final canto of "The Wasteland," The difference is that in Eliot the land is one totally of penance with a faint promise of salvation whereas in Lampman the nature of the land is more varied and the subtle balance evidence of more areas of promise.

In the third stanza, there is a shift in space, a movement closer to the poet, and a growing clarity of detail. The world of man with the exception of "the bridge" is gradually left behind and the use of the subjective "I" and "me" grows more frequent as we move into the natural world and eventually the poetic mind. The third stanza is crowded with three kinds of imagery, water, gold and light, and the circle. The sexual force of the sun is caught and the idea of the source of life is present in "soaks":

> Beyond me in the fields and sun
> Soaks in the grass and hath his will.

The sudden dwelling on the minutae of plant and insect and animal life reinforces the procreative powers of the sun and the earth. The colour white is contained in the marguerites, and gold and the circle in the buttercups. The last four lines revert to the aqueous world. "Cool" and "gloom" represent the modification of the negatives of the element of fire, cold and blackness. This is continued in the fourth stanza where the primary element and its negatives are placed side by side and the dependence of water in its life-giving form upon heat is emphasized:

94

> Where the far elm-tree shadows flood
> Dark patches in the burning grass.

The "peaceful cud" of the cows reinforces the conception of continuous movement in stillness. In the final four lines there is a concentrated image reiterating the two primary forms of the universe, the "slope" and perpetual revolution. The thrush also recalls other aspects of the typical poetic stance providing a direct link with the last stanza in the idea of "wandering"; "slope" is likewise returned to in the final stanza for a purpose which is eventually apparent. Stanzas five and six are the most objective. The line "In intervals of dreams I hear" provides more evidence that "dreams" had a precise meaning for the poet. By this time the creative imagination is engaged and at work so that the forms of external nature, the sights and sounds, are apparent only to the poet in "intervals." In the next line "droughty" returns to the desert idea. The singing of the grasshoppers suggests the creative possibilities for the artist of nature, the circle image, and unity in multiplicity. The sound is "innumerable." The line, "I lift mine eyes sometimes to gaze," with its Biblical overtones, brings to mind both the loss of physical sight and corresponding growth of spiritual illumination as in the poetry of Milton. The "burning skyline" blinds his physical eye and the distant woods are made indistinct with haze, but the symbol of the aspiring spirit, "the hills," are wondrously illuminated, the phrase "drenched with light" revealing the totality of perception in the fusion of the image of fire and water.

The opening two lines of the final stanza are stripped of metaphor and make an antithetical statement of the poem's concern which is caught up and dramatised in the varied image "summary" which concludes the poem. The two lines state the idea of unity in multiplicity, and of a poetic vision which must contend with the complexity and ambiguity of life, and indeed is content to do so:

> And yet to me not this or that
> Is always sharp or always sweet

"Sharp" is used here to mean sour. That is to say that life is not an occasion for the extremes of optimism or pessimism, that it is a mixture of joy and sorrow, triumph and tragedy. Moreover, "sharp" is developed in the last line to mean keenness of insight. By the next two lines the annihilating of the self as an identity separate from the world is complete. The poet takes on the shadow, and the circular image of the hat:

> In the sloped shadow of my hat
> I lean at rest, and drain the heat.

In "draining the heat" he is absorbing the force that has saturated nature, or possessing the meaning of heat, of the essence of life itself. This is why he can introduce the notion of a "blessed power," not something merely conventional because it really does appear that he has received a benediction in his insight.

We notice again the poetic stance in the paradox of the next line, a combination of apparently purposeless, purposive movement:

> Hath brought me wandering idly here.

The hour, the noon, has become a "furnace," and we can return now to my previous mention of Lampman's alchemical knowledge. A poem such as "Winter Evening" is full of metal imagery and something similar is implicit here. The furnace is the instrument for the melting, fusing, and transmutation of ore, the basic poetic material, into pure gold, complete poetic expression. Hence his:

> Thoughts grow keen and clear.

Keen is a word one associates with metal, with its cutting edge, with a weapon tempered to sharpness. The pen has become Lampman's sword and it is not too fanciful to suspect Lampman punning on the Latinate associations of "keen" as Marvell did in "An Horation Ode Upon Cromwell's Return From Ireland" with a similar playing upon acies, axe, or metal, and keenness or sharpness of insight. Likewise "clear" is precise in meaning, conveying lucidity and associated with the light which floods the poem in the same way "keen" is associated with the heat. In other words, Lampman is pointing out that his beliefs here have received complete poetic expression. The forms of nature, the poetic mind, and the poem itself are fused together in the re-creation of "divine and universal harmony."

At the very least, I believe it is possible to maintain that nature for Lampman was both a source of positive, organic values and an implicit criticism of the quality of a society increasingly de-humanized, tarnished, and cynical. He certainly did not use it as an escape from anything, but rather in his poetry it represents a quest, a struggle, affirmative and tragic, in which he sought to maintain a totality of response, a unified sensibility which fused intelligence, instinct, moral purpose, and imagination. In this way, we can appreciate the wholeness of his entire body of work and avoid the inconsistencies of many critics who express surprise that a poet who drugged his pain with nature could emerge from his dream to make direct attacks on contemporary society. If the nature poetry had been read more closely, it is unlikely that the two poems "Epitaph on a Rich Man" and "Liberty" would have appeared "like two mortar blasts" or would have revealed "an unexpected social awareness in Lampman." Nature for Lampman was synonymous with the possibilities of life, enabling easy recognition that "the shenanigans on Parliament Hill"[11] were some of the least subtle and least dangerous manifestations of what Lawrence called doing dirt on life.

NOTES

All page numbers in parentheses are taken from *The Poems of Archibald Lampman*, ed. with a Memoir by Duncan Campbell SCOTT (Toronto, 1905).

[1] Archibald LAMPMAN, "At the Mermaid Inn", Toronto *Globe*, Saturday, April 22, 1893.

[2] *Ibid.*

[3] Archibald LAMPMAN, "The Character and Poetry of Keats", ed. E. K. BROWN, *University of Toronto Quarterly*, 15 (July, 1946), p. 363.

[4] *The Complete Works of Percy Bysshe Shelley*, ed. INGPEN and PEEK, Vol X (New York, 1965), p. 26.

[5] H. D. THOREAU, *A Week on the Concord and Merrimack Rivers*, New American Library (New York, 1961), p. 325.

[6] Desmond PACEY, *Ten Canadian Poets* (The Ryerson Press, Toronto, 1958), p. 129.

[7] H. D. THOREAU, *Walden*, annotated with an introduction by Walter HARDING, Washington Square Press (New York, 1963), p. 160.

[8] Archibald LAMPMAN, "At the Mermaid Inn", Toronto *Globe*, Saturday, February 6, 1892.

[9] Desmond PACEY, *op. cit.*, p. 134.

[10] Archibald LAMPMAN, *At the Long Sault*, p. 26.

[11] See the review of *At the Long Sault* by Irving LAYTON in *First Statement*, Vol. 2, No. 5, (March, 1944).

BRUCE NESBITT

THE NEW LAMPMAN

Having been exposed to Robertson Davies' *Fifth Business* at far too young an age, I have been somewhat nervous about stones and rocks ever since. Indeed, I reread Doug Jones' *Butterfly on Rock* last month with a distinct sense of unease — as if I should be here today with lepidopterist's mouth, not butterflies in the stomach. For my theme is in part about being placed between a rock and a hard place, but there is irridescence in the spot: between Lampman's published texts and his manuscripts. And then *The Manticore* didn't lessen my sense of isolation, or its patterns, because I also have an instinctive mistrust of overtly psychoanalytic or biographical approaches to literature, and yet I am going to have to attempt some such readings of Lampman's newly revealed work, however superficially. My heart really lies with Robert G. Haliburton, Thomas's father, who obliquely commented on Charles Mair's verse in 1870 by noting that "Most Canadian poetry is still dominated by the sugary titles tacked on to them, such as 'Midnight Musings,' or, what is more to the point, 'Nocturnal Missions.' "[1] I feel rather like a colleague who asked me, when he saw me reading Pratt's war narrative *Behind the Log*, what I found there, behind it.

First to the rock: the texts we have understood to be Lampman's poetry. None but the pedant would begin at the end, and here I start, with "The City of the End of Things" and one miniscule example. All of us know the work, especially its apocalyptic — or nihilistic — conclusion in Tartarus, the place of punishment in Hades, with the three judges Aeacus, Minos and Rhadamanthus, and eventually Hades himself. There exists "a stillness absolute as death," when "The fires *shall* moulder out and die."[2] Or at least, some of us know it from the second edition of that anthology which we all respect greatly which properly dates the poem as *1889*, that of the poem's "first appearance in book form."[3] But what do we do with a new anthology published last year, which insists that the stillness is associated with "The fires *that moulder out and die*," and confidently reports (equally properly) that the text from which the selection was taken was published in *1900*?[4] "Shall" or "that"; 1899 or 1900? One word, and one year. Anyone here who thinks that one word or one year are unimportant would perhaps be happier in another room. What happened is obvious: the editors of the two anthologies chose different copy-texts. But how did the word get changed in that one year after Lampman's death?

A brief reminder about the publishing history of Lampman's first texts might be appropriate. Lampman himself saw his first three volumes at least to the proof stage: *Among the Millet*, which he had printed himself in Ottawa in 1888; *Lyrics of Earth*, 550 copies of which were published in Boston in March 1896 (although the edition is dated 1895), and *Alcyone*, set up in Edinburgh in 1899; Lampman died just after correcting the proofs, and his friend and literary executor Duncan Campbell Scott had a dozen copies printed from the standing type. These texts, then, we might assume to be sound. But it would be quite wrong to assume that those three volumes were simply reprinted in the memorial edition, the *Poems* of 1900, as its first three sections. Ominously, it is that collection which most Canadian scholars know best as the text for their commentary, and the one recently reprinted by the University of Toronto Press. As I have reported earlier, collation of the posthumous *Poems* with the earlier volumes reveals a disturbingly large number of accidental and substantive variants.[5] Summarized, they include changes in punctuation, grammatical and accentual alterations, inconsistency in spacing breaks and capitalisation, substitution of words, even the excision of an entire stanza. Duncan Campbell Scott, in all innocence, explained the source of the variants in his remarkable description of his work with E. K. Brown on the poems for the 1942 collection, *At the Long Sault*:

> they required some editorial attention, minor corrections of mere slips or errors in the pencilling, slight rearrangement here and there, and necessary punctuation. These editorial duties we have carried out as I did in preparing the Memorial Edition.[6]

(As an aside, I should add that although it is not generally appreciated, the plates for the text — but no other elements — of the memorial edition were used for the three further editions of the *Poems*, in 1901, 1905 and 1915. Apparent variants among these three later editions are due to type batter originating in the second [1901] edition. Even less known, it would seem, are the substantive changes evident in Scott's "Memoir" in the third and fourth editions when compared with the 1900 and 1901 version. The whole first page has been re-set to incorporate corrections. Interestingly, accidentals achieved by cutting the plates for the other pages involve only simple changes back to Canadian spelling conventions from the American spellings of the first two editions.) In other words, even on the evidence of Lampman's first three volumes, all students of Canadian literature should be aware that the 1900 memorial edition does not necessarily embody Lampman's final intentions. Since I have, unfortunately, thus disposed of nearly half of the received texts of Lampman's poetry, I have obviously to answer at least two further questions.

First, what of the poems in the memorial edition which were not published in his three earlier volumes (the ones Lampman himself corrected) but which were published in various magazines during his lifetime? This is more difficult, but it seems to me that he was rarely given the opportunity to correct proofs of those periodical publications, and in any case his correspondence suggests that he was highly vulnerable to the suggestions of editorial advisors. In a sense his texts were both victims of the nature of periodical publishing in North America during the late nineteenth century (a majority of these poems appear to have been first published in the United States); and victims of his lack of self-confidence in his own aesthetic judgement. Second, what of the unpublished poems which Scott chose for the memorial edition — forty-eight in all — together with the forty which he and E.K. Brown chose from Lampman's manuscripts to publish in *At the Long Sault* over four decades later, not to mention three others published elsewhere after Lampman's death. For the authority of these, too, we have had to accept the word of editors, and we have clear evidence that his editors (Scott, and later Scott and Brown), however wellmeaning, have not entirely given us Lampman. Let me state the proposition of the rock most clearly. I have made it before, but the newly reprinted combinatiion of the memorial edition and part of the *At the Long Sault* volume forces me to make it again. *No scholar can cite any single poem of Lampman's from any existing edition on the assumption that it is a pure text embodying Lampman's final intentions.* The proposition can be refined even further: generally speaking, *the published texts of Lampman's poetry are corrupt.*

If we are to recover Lampman, then, it is obvious that we have to turn to what I have called the hard place, rather than the rock: Lampman's manuscripts as we now have them and more particularly, his fair-copy manuscript books of poetry transcribed from his working papers. Seven manuscript books exist of which six are well-known: five in Ottawa, and one at the University of Toronto. Most of the contents of two of the six were published by Scott in the memorial edition: the fair-copy *David and Abagail* and *The Story of an Affinity*, both containing long narrative poems. Another fair-copy book is a selection of poems chosen by Lampman to represent approximately fifteen years of his writing. A further three are chronologically consecutive, including poems dated from 1883 to 1888, from 1889 to 1892, and from 1892 until 1899, the year of Lampman's premature death. And yet this last manuscript book is strangely rough, as if it represented a stage between his notebooks and fair-copy transcription. Several years ago my curiosity about the last book was further roused by the fact that in the memorial edition Scott included poems for which no manuscript versions had been uncovered. Could another, seventh, manuscrip book exist? As most of you now know, it does, as the result of a delightful instance of serendipity during my own research.[7] That volume, together with more than 100 of Lampman's letters to his fiancée and then wife, much other correspondence, photographs, a copy of *Alcyone*, and the original manuscript for his article on "The Character and Poetry of Keats" now comprises the Lampman Collection at Simon Fraser University.

Since then, my voyages in quest of the new Lampman, his poetry as he wrote it, have all too slowly taken me into numerous rocky coves, toward seductive bluffs and across all too many shallows. Endurance, of course, has been the key, through the thousands of pages of his notebooks, manuscript books, the fragmented bulk of his private correspondence with his wife and others, as well as his published and unpublished prose, and especially his more than twelve thousand lines of published poetry. Ten years ago I made available 3458 unpublished lines of Lampman's poetry;[8] since then I have added well over 1500 lines: in total, approximately one-third of Lampman's poetry which he expected or hoped to have published. The problem of how the future publication of this bulk of verse will affect our necessary reappraisal of Lampman is undoubtedly of some interest.

First, however, a small recantation is in order. From various sources, both public and private, many of us are aware that although he was married, Lampman was romantically involved with Katherine Waddell. The matter is complex. Arthur Bourinot helped clear the air in 1959 by publishing a letter from Duncan Campbell Scott to E. K. Brown, when they were working together on *At the Long Sault* in 1943. Referring to Lampman's surviving family (Bourinot records), Scott wrote that he had just "learned that they knew about the affair, and had given it a place in the life of A. L."[9] In fact Scott had actually said "that they knew about the affair, (that is too light a word to use) and had given it a place in the life of A. L."[10] After following this and several other suggestions, I wrote a note claiming that "it would be unsound to imply that Lampman's poetry was profoundly influenced by his friendship with Miss Waddell," although somewhat ambiguously, I did concede that his "letters and unpublished work suggest that Katherine Waddell's 'love and approbation' came to be his greatest hope, and their denial his most frustrating disillusionment."[11] I was wrong. Lampman's work *was* profoundly influenced by his *love* for Katherine Waddell, and I suggest that all his poetry written after 1892 has to be read with that knowledge. His unpublished poetry written during the fourteen years from 1878 to 1891 can from this perspective be considered separately from that written in the last eight years of his life, from 1892 to 1899. Slightly more than half of his unpublished poems belong to this latter period, when he was battling his "emotional demon" and undergoing a "spiritual revolution." That other work which we now know well was suppressed is obvious from the publication of *At the Long Sault*, which appeared forty-four years after Lampman's death. More remains,[12] but I wish to emphasize that my point is not simple teasing or titillation. When one attempts a complete edition of a poet's works, the responsibility of attempting to enter another person's mind, however peripherally, is fearsome, chilling and humbling.

Of Lampman's earlier unpublished poetry, most has remained in manuscript because Lampman didn't wish to have it published at a particular time, or because he realised that he couldn't get it printed except at his own expense, despite the common practice of publishing by subscription. Some, of course, is juvenilia, or banal in the sense that it failed to meet even his somewhat insecure aesthetic standards. Or again, he was discouraged by friends or editors whom he chose to believe. And so, or because of these, his longest poem of 1184 lines ("Arnulph") which took him thirteen months to complete, or "White Margaret," of 753 lines (but which apparently occupied only 14 days of his time) remain entombed primarily as manuscript documents in late nineteenth-century literary imitation, albeit perpetrated by a sensitive observor (and reflector) of educated Canadian taste. A handful are trials, fragments, or cancels. The omission of several from his canon are simply inexplicable. "Storm and Purpose," for instance, from January 1883, and "January," dated February 1884, are both important statements which amplify what I consider to be some of his most significant concerns about the relationship of man and his environment. Equally if not more significant is one poem, "The Vagrant," from 1884, an aesthetic experiment which to my mind is also one of the earliest and strongest intimations of what has come to be called rather condescendingly his pale or Fabian socialism. I have little doubt that it was consciously suppressed, in the same sense that he later left a not unsimilar poem, "Reality,", buried in the Toronto *Globe*: because it offended the almost monolithic opposition among readers of the time to work which could be seen to attack the prevailing sentiments about moral earnestness. Since this aspect of Lampman's writing has attracted some attention recently, it might not be out of order for me to mention one poem by John Henry Brown, a clerk in the Post Office Department at the same time as Lampman, whose *Poems: Lyrical and Dramatic*, published in Ottawa in 1892, have faded from view. With the obvious models — particularly Whitman — in mind, Brown began a verse search for "eternal values," "Looking Forward," by vowing that he will

> ...look backward, I will imagine enchanted
>   bowers, palaces, ladies and knights.
> I will escape the commonplace,
> I will dwell in the impalpable, dreaming sweet dreams.

Suddenly, Brown tells us,

> ...the purpose of life was changed.
> I looked on the world and accepted it;
> Accepted the common, the gross, the dull;
> No more wished to be of the elect;
> No more wished to stand with eyes turned backward or
>   in the clouds;
> To dream dreams, to surfeit with perfumed fancies.[13]

But Brown's ostensibly iconoclastic attack on Lampman's *Among the Millet* (or so I take it), however indirect, misses its point as unerringly as Wilfrid Campbell's delightful satirical verse on Lampman's style, "At Even," hits his.[14] For while Campbell lights on what he regarded as the total inappropriateness of Lampman's experimentation with realistic diction, Brown reveals that he *accepts* the reality of "the common, the gross, the dull." However idealistically, Lampman hoped to *change* the gross and the dull by describing it aesthetic possibilities at first, and eventually by stimulating a moral awakening among Canadians. Nevertheless that Lampman's dreaming was the object of public satire as early as 1892 is significant, as a noteworthy example of a complete misunderstanding of his intellectual schema which would persist for at least another generation.

When we turn to Lampman's later unpublished poetry, that written after 1892, however, the question of why some poetry was not published or why Lampman chose not to have some poetry published becomes very difficult indeed. It is clear that all the verses of social protest which Scott and E. K. Brown collected in *At the Long Sault* come from this period — in fact I have been able to discover only three poems which can be considered to be social protest and which were written before 1892. As I have explained elsewhere, I am convinced that Lampman's affair with Katherine Waddell heightened his personal instability to the point where he undertook, consciously or not, a complete re-evalution of his relationship with his society, both personally and in his poetry. But at the same time, his bitter verses directed against the human flaws of that society (not the institutional ones, it should be noted) were too bitter for his contemporaries.

Of material which remained unpublished at his death, two longer poems may serve as examples of the significance of the peculiar autobiographical element which came to dominate nearly all his work of the 1890s. Both are dated 1893. The first, "Sebastian," or "The Mill Hand," describes a vigorously physical man, a worker in a saw mill, whose vision embraces both the turbulence of the logs, river and mill, and the nearby city, with its "mingled sough and tumult of mankind, / Groping forward toward an unseen end." "Brain, flesh and spirit" are melded in him as he increases his knowledge by reading, until with a sense of anticipation, he reaches a state which finds him triumphantly "Lonely, self-centred, pure, and armed with joy," ready for an unnamed encounter, having "seen the god," his own ultimate potential. The second, "The Settler's Tale," tells of a man of the north whose digging of three graves patterns the loss first of his wife, who is his love, then of his daughter, who is the psychological fruit and hope of his love and finally of his soul, the force which gave meaning to his commitment. He is rescued from a form of suicide, after a violent storm tumbles him into his own, third, grave by an Indian, and he concludes by declaring:

> You see I am bred in a bitter school:
> I am not as other men are, a pool,

> That shrieks in the onrush of every beast,
> But smiles and is still, when the tempest is past.[15]

The "beast," I suggest, is the same one he condemns in "Life and Death": sheer lust, as opposed to the ineffable spirit which allows safety only to the man who learns "to house himself in thought, and feel."[16]

And yet throughout these and several other poems is a curious sense of distancing, of psychological impotence, as in "My Master's Daughter." That the mysterious grey-eyed woman of the poem is Katherine Waddell is obvious: "A dreaming witch, half hard, half week [sic]." The speaker, a retainer in a noble family, is drawn to her "with a mingled power / Of passion and of dread"; were she even to look on him "My startled spirit would break loose, / My madness have its way":

> But God who made and fashioned me
> With every mortal need,
> Left not a single byway free
> To any natural deed.

These intimations of eunuchism are noteworthy (and significant for having been left unpublished), because they are followed almost immediately by a characteristic attitude of Lampman's:

> But some time in the end this strife
> Must pass and leave me free:
> Only the dream shall stand like life,
> The sole reality.

The light this casts on his concept of the dream I will comment on in a moment, but here it is important that he concludes much in the terminology of moral uplift: at some time he will be "safe sheltered and beyond the stress / Of conflict or despair."[17] Again in 1893, but uncharacteristically projecting himself into the feminine half of a thwarted relationship in "Margaret," the poet has an agonized and beautiful woman ask "Whose the blame was — his or hers":

> Was her own response too chill
> To his once impassioned call?

And yet once more Lampman insists on offering a compensating explanation: Margaret shall arise from the experience "anew," "remade," "divine" even.[18] On the other hand, three years later in 1896, Lampman appears to have been struck by the possibilities of neater conclusions. In "Katrina d'Amatrice" the author is once more inferior to his master, a painter, and his mistress, "the stronger of the two." While travelling on the road, they are beset by marauders; Katrina, with becoming modesty, recognises that "my beauty is the prize that brings / Their clamour at such speed." Spreading her arms, she leaps from a cliff, and the men (although humiliated) are spared.[19] In "Jelina," we again find an enchantingly beautiful queen; so beautiful, in fact, that modern readers should not be misled by the poet's statement that "all the minstrels of those days / Took Queen Jelina for their lays." Puzzled by the disappearance of his two young brothers, both of whom had vowed to win the queen's hand, one Buk surreptitiously enters Jelina's castle. There her beauty snares him, and he is "fettered body and soul; / His judgment and his will she stole." It turns out that she is a man-eater, playing with her suitors "till I was satisfied," and then casting them off a cliff. Buk takes his revenge, however, not by pushing Queen Jelina off the cliff, but by seizing her in his arms and jumping off himself, carrying her with him.[20] The idea of fatal possession, then, was clearly one which strongly influenced Lampman's views on human relationships, and which has a clear link to his writing verse dramas under his "impulse."

So far I have deliberately concentrated on Lampman's longer unpublished poems and verse drama because I believe that many of these works, together with "The Story of an Affinity," can reveal to us part of the dark turbulence of Lampman's mind during years when he was writing powerful and occasionnally exquisite poetry of a wholly different kind. And I have not wanted to lead you into a mistaken inference that my work in preparing a definitive edition of Lampman's poems will bring forth a vast body of unknown material of the quality, say, of *At the Long Sault*, however uneven the accomplishment recorded there. Yet there is some very good poetry in the unknown third of Lampman, just as there is some very bad verse, and a large amount of what might be called fair average quality Lampman. I apologise for the critical travesty which that statement represents, buy obviously I would be perpetrating even more critical absurdities were I to attempt to summarize my views on the large number of shorter poems, the fragments of nearly completed work, and particularly the numerous stanzas which were deleted from poems familiar to us all, but not deleted by Lampman. My more immediate concluding purpose is to justify the title I gave this discussion, "the new Lampman."

Allow me three incidental propositions, and some interim observations. First, Lampman is undeniably Canada's finest nineteenth-century poet. Second, the evidence by which we can judge his importance to Canadian literature is at the moment grossly inadequate. Margaret Whitridge's annotated cheklist of Lampmania was an invaluable beginning to serious scholarly understanding, but that we should still lack a substantial biography in the seventh decade after his death indicates the infancy of our studies. Third, Canadian universities, with only three or four exceptions, have been scandalously neglectful in failing to encourage studies which are essential to our understanding of nineteenth-century Canadian literary and intellectual history.

Now some observations. If I am right, or even partly so, about the influence of Lampman's personal life on his poetry, particularly his poetry of social protest and his verse dramas, have I in effect been a retrograde revisionist, reducing the former to mere Christian humanism, and the latter to self-indulgent exercises in psychotherapy? I think not.

If I have appeared so far to have ignored Lampman's response to his natural environment, it is because only now is it suitable for me to suggest a point which has long pre-occupied me: Lampman's contribution to the development of the Canadian literary imagination. I suggest that Lampman, first among Canadian poets, both defined and accomplished the break between what has been called colonial romanticism on the one hand, and a variety of close-focussed poetic imagism on the other, a form of poetry which articulated whatever would come to be accepted as the essence of Canadian poetry in the generation or two after him. The way Lampman linked language and environment is in my view the most important development in English Canadian poetry before 1936 and the appearance of *New Provinces.* Two provocative observations by John Matthews may be helpful, both made about Lampman's "Heat." First, he suggests that "nature, in its extremes, allows man to recognize his own powers, and shows.... that he can make of it what he will... nature's main virtue llies in its ability to provide a setting where man may strip away the artificial barriers that bar the way to self-knowledge." Second, "endurance against nature's extremes becomes, thus, not mere stoicism, but an active moral and humanistic principle."[21] I would argue that Lampman's poetic technique is essentially dualistic, and inclusively dualistic rather than intrusive; he does not erect barriers between an urban and natural environment, for instance, but sees them together. Further, his "intension," what George Whalley has called the poet's "impulsive orientation... in a moment of awareness," is trinitarian.[22] As in "Morning on the Lièvre," the forest and the stream "meet and plight," with the poet as celebrant, all wrapped in a "dream." I would argue that in his most considered uses of the term, his "dream" is the process by which poetic, and therefore human knowledge is realised. It is a condition of stasis in which all forces operating on man are comprehended, and during which the poet has visions of man's ideal condition. These visions lead to a direct confrontation with the forces — such as materialism — which would bind his soul. Persistent struggle with them may result in self-knowledge, the realisation of his identity. And as several of Lampman's poems suggest, unfallen nature becomes a symbol of Christ's endurance, just as her extremes suggest to man the struggle he must inevitably endure if he is to be man. Thus Lampman's apparent escape into nature is actually the first step to man's integration with himself and a regenerated society. In a sense Lampman attempts to literalise the myth of the loss of identity, the expulsion from Eden, for a nation unwilling or unable to accept its metaphorical basis.[23] The conclusion of his unpublished "Storm and Purpose," dated as early as January 1883 suggests much of this argument exceptionally clearly:

To the wild white wastes and bitter weather,
To the howling blasts that break and flee,
Round the mighty pines that laugh together,
Tossing in the storm's face, and are free,

> From mean words and meaner thoughts that fret me
> From the home of labour and dull pain,
> I will go and clasp the storm, and get me
> Comfort for dreams dead, and dream again.[24]

And so ten years later we are scarcely surprised to find in the unpublished "Out of the Cities" the three last stanzas:

> I think the wind is the mightiest voice,
>   One of the words of fate;
> It saith to the people each and all:
>   Be rugged, be iron, and wait.

> For the tides of passion surge and flow
>   Like my voice from either hand,
> And only he who hath steeled his heart
>   Can hold to his life and stand.

> Only he hath steeled his heart,
>   And knoweth his own soul well; —
> He shall look upon heaven with equal eyes,
>   And ride by the gates of hell.[25]

Yet here is no reference to dream, dead or otherwise. Instead we see, if you will, the dream at work, the process itself, the artifact, the poem. Both heaven and hell are here as words, just as we may also sense behind the words that the writing of the poem was both heaven and hell for Lampman. Not a catharsis, but the struggle. The intellectual constructs underlying his poetry, the theory of the dream I have briefly outlined above, suddenly has become a continuing reality, and endless struggle. More disturbing, it seems to me that Lampman was appalled at what self-knowledge he did gain as a result of his love for Katherine Waddell. In the strongest possible sense, for Lampman literature had become life. After 1892, put another way, his writing was both his vision and his struggle.

When I referred earlier to John Henry Brown's apparent attack on Lampman, some of you may have been reminded of A. J. M. Smith's definition of colonial romanticism in literature, a definition now over thirty years old, but one which still has some validity:

> Colonialism is a spirit that gratefully accepts a place of subordination, that looks elsewhere for its standards of excellence and is content to imitate with a modest and timid conservatism the products of the parent tradition.... One of the most damaging of the results of pure colonialism is the feeling of inferiority and doubt it engenders and the remoteness it encourages. Thus a direct result of colonialism may be a turning away from the despised local present not towards the mother country but towards an exotic idealized crystallization of impossible hopes and "noble" dreams. The romantic spirit, indeed, is encouraged by a colonial spirit of inferiority.[26]

If any of Lampman's work deserves the tag of colonial romanticism, one might say, it is surely what he called "those tales in verse."[27] And indeed, of his thirteen poems over 200 lines long (three of them unpublished), only two are even set in Canada. The others include the Luddite and Utopian "Land of Pallas"; two set in ancient Greece, one in Biblical Israel, one in Christ's Judea, one in immediately post-Christian Rome, one in Eddic Norway, and two each in England and Italy of the Middle Ages: a thoroughly Romantic and amorous quest of the far past. Moreover, in each of these imaginative recreations, Lampman consciously heightens his diction. Altitudinizing becomes the dominant mood. What E. J. Pratt once called "O Thouing" is the rule. All evidence suggests that at the same time he was writing poetry which exhibits few or none of these characteristics. His turning from the thing perceived to the thing imagined and back again is extraordinarily marked and strangely constant.

I have, in effect, been suggesting that a rather vague concept of distancing is involved in colonial romanticism. From what I have said earlier, I should perhaps now be expected to suggest that after his involvement with Miss Waddell, it was essential for Lampman to distance himself from his immediate surroundings, even from his usual diction, because otherwise much of this writing might be for him too real, too autobiographical, too painful. And yet I must now turn much of the direction of the logic of my discussion upside down. I have made a strong claim for an alteration in Lampman's perception of his relationships with the outside world, one associated with his love for Miss Waddell. But given the context of this immediate point it is reasonably clear to me that the essential differences between his "tales in verse" and his "nature work, as they call it,"[28] were not substantially affected by the upheaval in his personal life. That is, I suggest that the concept of Lampman's dual sensibilities gains force precisely because it does not appear to have been affected by the most disturbing element of his personal life. His dual styles, then, were not the results of momentary aberrations in literary taste, or of catering to popular sales, but rather were integral parts of his bifurcated, syncretic world-view. When Lampman attempted his narratives of noble dreams, he felt obliged to imitate the parent tradition, both in what to see and how to feel. When he turned to the country around him, he dropped that particular form of his assumed poetic baggage. He may not have abondoned all his Keatsian diction or Emersonian assumptions but with that diction he expressed attitudes neither colonial nor romantic (nor wholly trancendentalist, for that matter). No amount of revision could alter the dual sensibilities of Lampman. He had defined the break with colonial romanticism. The signifiance of his accomplishment went unrecognized, but its substance would be recaptured by W. W. E. Ross, and especially Frank Scott. As Lampman predicted in "Man's Future," time forward would be discovered not through the "rhythmic whole" but through the "long adjustment." He is still with us.

NOTES

[1] Queen's University, Mair Papers, Haliburton to Mair, 24 August 1870, quoted in J. P. MATTHEWS, *Tradition in Exile* (Toronto: University of Toronto Press, 1962), p. 99.

[2] C. F. KLINCK and R. E. WATTERS, edd., *Canadian Anthology* (Rev. ed.; Toronto: Gage, 1966), p. 129. My italics.

[3] "Preface to the revised edition", *ibid.*, [1].

[4] Catherine McLAY, ed., *Canadian Literature: The Beginnings to the 20th Century* (Toronto: McClelland and Stewart, 1974), p. 295. My italics.

[5] "Lampmania: Alcyone and the Search for Merope" in F. G. HALPENNY, ed., *Editing Canadian Texts* (Toronto: Hakkert, 1975).

[6] "Foreword" to *At the Long Sault and Other New Poems by Archibald Lampman* (Toronto: Ryerson, 1943), p. ix.

[7] See "Lampmania" in HALPENNY, *op. cit.*, pp. 42 ff.

[8] In an Appendix to *Lampman and O'Dowd* (Queen's University, unpublished M. A. thesis, 1965), pp. 110-273. Since then, I have revised some attributions; at the time, Lampman's notebooks had not been acquired by the National Library.

[9] Scott to Brown, 18 January 1943, in Arthur S. BOURINOT, ed., *Some Letters of Duncan Campbell Scott..., Archibald Lampman & Others* (Ottawa: A. S. Bourinot, 1959), p. 22.

[10] Public Archives of Canada, E.K. Brown Papers, Scott to Brown, 18 January 1943.

[11] "A Gift of Love: Lampman and Life", *Canadian Literature,* no. 50. (1971).

[12] Margaret Coulby WHITRIDGE'S *Lampman's Kate: Late Love Poems of Archibald Lampman, 1887-1897* (Ottawa: Borealis Press, 1975) is an important addition. Appearing concurrently with the Symposium, the collection is not considered here.

[13] *Poems: Lyrical and Dramatic* (Ottawa: J. Durie, 1892), pp. 100-101.

[14] *The Globe* (Toronto), 1 July 1893, in Arthur S. BOURINOT, ed., *At the Mermaid Inn* (Ottawa: A.S. Bourinot, 1958), p. 94

[15] Simon Fraser University Library, Lampman Collection, 1893-1897 MS Book, f. 8.

[16] *Ibid.*, f. 45.

[17] *Ibid.*, ff. 13-14.

[18] *Ibid*, ff. 31-32.

[19] *Ibid.*, ff. 119-122.

[20] *Ibid.*, ff. 125-127.

[21] *Op. cit.*, pp. 124-125.

[22] "Introduction" to *Poetic Process* (London: Routledge and Kegan Paul, 1953), n. 1 to p. xxvii.

[23] For an early and more detailed examination of these suggestions, see my *Lampman and O'Dowd* (1965), pp. 29-69 and 98-104.

[24] Public Archives of Canada, Lampman Papers, *Miscellaneous Poems*, f. 14.

[25] Simon Fraser University Library, Lampman Collection, 1893-1897 MS Book, f. 18.

[26] "Colonialism and Nationalism in Canadian Poetry Before Confederation", Canadian Historical Association, *Report*, 1944, pp. 74-75.

[27] Lampman to E. W. Thomson, 22 November 1893, in Arthur S. BOURINOT, ed., *Archibald Lampman's Letters to E. W. Thomson 1890-1898)* (Ottawa: A. S. Bourinot, 1956), p. 23.

[28] *Ibid.*

SANDRA DJWA

LAMPMAN'S ACHIEVEMENT

Listening to the papers of the last two days, my strongest impression is that we are just beginning to put together the information essential for evaluating Lampman's achievement. There are at least three problems arising from our discussions which might be considered.

The first point relates to Lampman's attitude to nature. Was he, as some earlier critics have claimed, an idle dreamer, an escapist from human society and is this attitude related to a form of Platonism similar to that discussed by Professor Barrie Davies? Or was he, as Professor Carl Klinck has convincingly argued, an Emersonian transcendentalist, for whom union with the Immensity and All led to a greater understanding of self and of communion with his fellow man? The Emersoniam hypothesis, when considered in additon to influences from the English Romantic poets, would accommodate Lampman's insistence upon the perceiving eye, his emphasis on whim, his passiveness in nature, his anti-intellectualism. Most importantly, it would provide a justification for a system of correspondences between man and nature. As such, Emersonian idealism would minimize the retreat inherent in nature worship by insisting that such experiences enlarge the poet's understanding of himself and his fellow man; in Lampman's metaphor, his experiences in nature are not only poetic "dream" but also "true reality."

But if Lampman's attitude to nature in "The Frogs" is to be explained with reference to Emersonian idealism, at what stage did he adopt his philosophy? His interest in the frogs as emissaries of nature's truth is to be found in his work as early as 1885 in "Hans Fingerhut's

111

Frog Lesson." But there the mortal must undergo metamorphosis — that is, actually become a frog — in order to understand the correspondences between the natural order and the universal order. What he comes to accept with the cosmic (if coy) "Song of the Water Drops" is a providential interpretation of the great sea of being. It is possible that Lampman is attempting to counter Victorian and personal pessimism by providing a fairy tale solution to the melancholy withdrawing sea of Matthew Arnold's "Dover Beach" — a sea which in the larger context of Arnold's poetry signifies both the sea of faith and the buried life. We do know that Lampman was emotionally depressed at that time:

> I am in the midst now of the barren period; I cannot work; I have been writing at a voluminous fairy tale.... I have been very dull and out of spirits. — oppressed with innumerable things — debts; ill-success in everything, incapacity to write and want of any hopes of ever succeeding in it if I do. I cannot do anything — I believe I am the feeblest and most good-for-nothing mortal any where living.... I wrote another fairy tale the other day.

The emphasis on actual metamorphosis that we find in "Hans Fingerhut's Frog Lesson" is repeated in a similar fairy tale, "The Fairy Fountain," that Lampman was apparently writing simultaneously. This tale also emphasizes a series of metamorphoses and concludes as does "Hans Fingerhut," with a stoical acceptance of man's lot in life.

Did Lampman, as did Wilfred Campbell, turn to Emersonian transcendentalism as a solution to his unhappiness of 1885? If so, this might lead to the transcendental "exercises" on nature's dream and the frogs which Professor Klinck finds in the sonnet sequence "The Frogs." But is it also possible that a generation of university students persist in reading "The Frogs" and the later poem "The Favourites of Pan" (in which Pan is described as passing on the poetic voice to the frogs) at mythic face value because much of the early Lampman — the pretty pagan pantheism of the school boy who would have read Ovid's *Metamorphoses* and the young university student who read Roberts' *Orion* (1880) which he praised for its "pagan earth-loving Greekish flavour" — still remained.

Secondly, what was Lampman's religious position? Professor Davies' paper on the reflections of Platonism, Emerson and Hinduism in Lampman's poetry was very helpful and we might query the relation of this information to that other aspect of Lampman's religious consciousness — a predilection for the suffering Christ as a kind of reinstated "Pale Galilean". We find an approval of suffering and masochistic pain in "Viva Perpetua" and "Chione" and a justification of martyrdom in the sonnet "The Martyrs." One of Lampman's most striking poems on the subject of human evil is the account of the burning of the three Christians in "The Three Pilgrims." How do we reconcile the mordibity of these poems with the optimism of transcendentalism, Hinduism and Plantonism? And what about his other 'ism' — socialism? What books and topics were discussed at the Ottawa Fabrian Club and were there specific reflections of these and further readings in Lampman's poems? More importantly, whether he was a serious socialist or not, to what extent does his socialist verse succeed as poetry? "To a Rich Man," for example, is good socialism but poor verse.

Finally, there is the problem of the collecting of the Lampman canon and the attitude we are to take to textual revisions by D. C. Scott and E.K. Brown. In the first instance, we owe a debt of gratitude to Margaret Whitridge, whose pioneering scholarship has resulted in a comprehensive bibliography of Lampman's work; a new printing of *The Poems of Arhibald Lampman* (1974); and *Lampman's Kate* (1975), hitherto unavailable love poems. From a reading of much of the unpublished verse, I would suspect that we now have the best of Lampman's work. In any event, the re-evaluation that may come from a new edition of Professor Bruce Nesbitt's restored Lampman may not be quite what we imagine. A comparison between the manuscript copy of "At the Long Sault" and the published version reveals that the poem has been considerably improved by D. C. Scott's deft editing. By the shifting of a few lines, the indentation of some others, the changing of a few words — "burg" becomes "town," for example — Scott has removed those awkwardnesses in form and diction which spoil the poem. As the poem existed in manuscript copy and was not finished at Lampman's death, and as Lampman regularly allowed Scott to make such changes, I would view this action as a final collaboration between friends. Certainly, Scott believed this. In his correspondence to E. K. Brown, contained in the Public Archives, he clearly delineated changes made and comments that he has not made any changes that he would not have suggested to Lampman when alive.

Consequently, I anticipate that the task of editing a definitive Lampman will be a difficult one: to what extent should one accept editorial emendations to rough copy such as punctuation revision; to what extent should one accept simultaneous changes in diction and prosody? As we have seen with reference to "At the Long Sault," the sad fact is that the restored Lampman may very well be a lesser Lampman. There are few of us who will be able to bring ourselves to recite "Behind them the sleepless dream / Of the little frail walled burg." As the D. C. Scott version of the poem is the superior one and as the poem is currently accepted in its present form, considerable editorial tact is required. In cases of this sort, annotation which recognizes changes but allows them to stand might be indicated.

Given then what we have learned in the past two days, and given the canon which we have, how do we evaluate Archibald Lampman's achievement and his contribution to Canadian poetry? G. H. Unwin's 1917 description of Lampman as "a native genius, moulded and ripened by a study of the masters of English verse, but distinctively fresh and Canadian" is perhaps a good a description as any. English verses, in this context, might be taken to include American verse and so signify the varying influences from both traditions. "Distinctively fresh and Canadian" is a clear reference to Lampman's nature poetry and he is undoubtedly our first "native genius." It is his early poetry, where the perceiving eye and poetic process coalesce, that I find most satisfying.

> How still it is here in the woods. The trees
>   Stand motionless, as if they did not dare
>   To stir, lest it should break the spell. The air
> Hangs quiet as spaces in a marble frieze.
> Even this little brook, that runs at ease,
>   Whispering and gurgling in its knotted bed,
>   Seems but to deepen, with its curling thread
> Of sound, the shadowy sun-pierced silences.
> Sometimes a hawk screams or a woodpecker
>   Startles the stillness from its fixed mood
> With his loud carelesse tap. Sometimes I hear
>   The dreamy white-throat from some far off tree
> Pipe slowly on the listening solitude
>   His five pure notes succeeding pensively.

D.G. JONES

LAMPMAN'S ACHIEVEMENT

Archibald Lampman's achievement was to articulate many of the elements that were to be central to the English-Canadian imagination for the next two or three generations — both in terms of its decor and in terms of its structure.

By locating the images of desire in the intimate experience of a semi-cultivated nature and the images of fear in the proliferating urban, commercial and industrial world, Lampman reverses the dominant pattern of nineteenth century writing and defines the poles of the imaginative landscape as it still emerges in the work of a George Grant, Dennis Lee, Margaret Laurence, Margaret Atwood, Dale Zeiroth or Tom Wayman.

In dissociating himself from the main collective enterprise of his society, Lampman explores an ironic position between pessimism and optimism, between a short term sense of individual isolation and a long term ideal of· collective development — the latter finding its most political definition in Lampman's socialism. This has been the characteristic position of many Canadian artists and intellectuals in the twentieth century.

But let us start with the obvious and most particular. Lampman, the "nature poet," was foremost in beginning the detailed inventory of the kind of natural landscape that, more than any social or urban landscape, would furnish the remembered images of pleasure and desire and define an essential part of the sensibility of many English-Canadians. It is a world of dusty summer roads and winter uplands, of woodlots and open fields, of waterbugs and daisies and white-throat sparrows, blue jays and mullein stalks, autumn ducks and winter chickadees. "The Frogs," "Heat," "Solitude," "November," "Winter Evening," "A January Morning," all define moods that many of us recognize.

George Grant has said that the encounter with the land was primal in the experience of Canadians, at least until the sixties. It was primal for Lampman, not in the instrumental or conditional sense it might have had for Crawford's pioneer of Grove's prairie farmer or Pratt's railway builder, but in the definitive sense it had for James Reaney when he speaks of the Thames and the country around Straford, Ontario as having defined for him, once and for all, the meaning of star, snow, river, world. For Frank Scott it was the Laurentian hills stretching away to the north from his father's yard in Quebec City, picnics on the Saguenay, summers spent in Lachute or in the Eastern Townships. For Earle Birney it was the Kootenays and B.C.'s forests and mountains. For Raymond Souster it was Toronto Island and the rolling country north of the city. For Irving Layton it was the Laurentian foothills. For Purdy, Prince Edward County, the Bay of Quinte, and the "Country North of Belleville." For Margaret Atwood, Lake Kipawa and the country around Temiscaming. For many Canadians it was just this kind of natural world that furnished an important part of the decor of their inner world, defining certain moods, feeding their pastoral dreams.

The decor that Lampman articulates finds its most immediate echo in readers from Ontario and Quebec. He draws on his boyhood knowledge of the countryside around Rice Lake, between Peterborough and Port Hope. Here he provides a certain continuity between the earliest articulate experience of the Stricklands, Mrs. Moodie and Mrs. Traill, and perhaps Isabella Crawford, and that of Margaret Laurence in her recent novel, *The Diviners*. Later Lampman knew something of the country around Toronto and Orangeville. Obviously, much of his work speaks directly of his experience of the world of the Ottawa Valley, to a slighter degree of the St. Lawrence, more surely of the Gatineau, and in its extreme limits of Algonquin Park, Temagami and Lake Temiscamingue. This is the world that furnished Lampman with his images of whatever was delightful, vital, awesome. It could also furnish the elements that defined feelings of loneliness, melancholy, something verging on anguish. But as long as he drew on this area of his experience, he at least felt real.

√ It is the "unreal city" that furnishes the demonic or nightmare side of Lampman's vision. It provides images of confusion and violence, hostility and isolation, as in the ironically titled "Reality." But the main point is, that however intensely vivid or irritating such urban and social situations may be, Lampman has difficulty according them a convincing reality. Their pure conventionality or dynamic selfishness or vapid technism ensure that the actors will be cut off from any more profound life or essential and unifying reality. It is the essential vacuity of such a world that characterizes the nightmare vision of "The City of the End of Things."

Certainly it is easier to argue that Lampman defined the demonic pole of the English-Canadian imagination as it has haunted us down to the present day, where it has begun to haunt French-Canadians as well. It does not have the same moral colouring as Baudelaire's unreal city, nor the cultural and spiritual overtones of Eliot's wasteland, or the violence of Ginsberg's Moloch. It is a modest Canadian nightmare, but its horror is finally the same. In general, it anticipates a whole tradition of Canadian writers since, Birney's view of the city in "The Way West," Layton's in "The Improved Binoculars," Souster's in multiple images of Toronto, Avison's in "The Local and the Lakefront," Newlove's or Wayman's or Zeiroth's in various poems, or David Helwig in his poem "Cities," which begins, "We name them as a way of naming death." Increasingly the "unreal" landscape is our common inheritance as twentieth century human beings.

Lampman's "real" landscape, however, has certain features which may allow it to speak more generally for all Canadians, not just those on the Laurentian fringe of Ontario and Quebec. It is primarily the semi-cultivated world of nature lying between the exclusively urban metropolis and the extreme wilderness. And one of its fundamental verities is the cyclical rhythm of the seasons. And the key season, in which he symbolically centers his perspective, is Fall.

W. L. Morton has developed a whole historical interpretation of the Canadian experience, of the Canadian identity, around the idea that the basic rhythm of Canadian life is determined by a movement out into the hinterland to gather staples and raw materials — fur, fish, lumber, pulp, minerals, oil — and back to the metropolis, from the violent and crude to the genteel and refined, and that this movement is both symbolized and governed by the rhythm of the seasons. To this extreme oscillation between winter and summer, nature and culture, he ascribes a characteristic Canadian reserve, cautiousness, puritanism. He might have added, a certain irony.

Lampman was quite aware of these two extremes, but he tended to locate himself in a kind of middle ground — for a long time the typical and rather tenuous middle ground of many Canadians who provided the local supporting base for the economy and tried to live as an independent society. It is typically the middle ground that Roberts looked back upon with childhood nostalgia in "Tantramar Revisited" and, more sombrely, in "The Sower" as well as in many poems in *Songs of the Common Day*. It is the middle ground Purdy resurrects in "The Country North of Belleville" and in his peripatetic meditations around Roblin Lake. It is the world of Reaney's *Twelve Letters to a Small Town*. It is Newlove's Verigin, Nowlan's Hartland and Stoney Ridge, Pat Lane's B.C. interior.

More simply and certainly Robert Kroetsch has spoken of the ironic situation of the Canadian, who sits Januslike between the most highly urban and industrial society the world has known, just to the south, and one of the few remaining wilderness areas, stretching away on a continental scale, just to the north — between a great noise and a great silence. These are the poles established by Lampman's noisy but negative "Reality" and his silent but positive "Solitude." And it remains largely the two poles of Dennis Lee's "Civil Elegies," which plays throughout on the ambiguous, positive and negative possibilities of the word "void."

More than most, Lampman's work might be arranged on the principal of the calendar. Seasonal rhythms are one of the absolutes of his world. In a general way he begins with spring and ends with winter. He begins with the outer sun awakening the frogs and soaking the fields; he ends with an inner sun holding its own against the night and snow, keeping him wrapped against the cold. The season of balance is late autumn and winter, the season of irony, of a double perspective.

The Canadian has seldom been able to rest in any single perspective without being quickly challenged by another. However rooted or convinced of the truth of his own sensations, he has had to mediate between British and American, French and English, East and West, Old World wisdom and New World science, action and meditation. One may think of Irving Layton's "Vexata Quaestio," or of Margaret Avison's "Meeting of Poles and Latitudes (in Prospect)." John Moss has remarked that irony is probably the inevitable result of any really objective awareness in a country like Canada, and he maintains that its fictional heroes are characterized precisely by an ironic awareness that measures the degree of their isolation and makes of them, neither social leaders nor recluses, but merely individuals. Lampman is ironic in just this sense. And so are most Canadian poets from his day to the present.

I cannot read individual poems, or even a whole collection by David Helwig without being reminded of Lampman, in details of the decor or in its ironic structure. I come across similar echoes in George Johnston, particularly in the later poetry as Johnston moves away from the city.

Take the case of Frank Scott, who led the revolt against Lampman and the Confederation poets. Scott is much wittier than Lampman, but the targets of his satire are the same, and the sense of civic duty and collective concern are the same, and the democratic socialism they envision for their society is the same. Scott tends to discount the private individual self in the interests of collective action and progress; he would have us recognize the avant-garde and participate in the march of events; yet he may become fascinated by the Mackenzie, a river that turns its back on America. Scott has a more optimistic faith in reason and action and technology, but the more he moves out into space in the technological adventure, the more he is also drawn back to a memory of moonlight on a cold Laurentian lake — and its paradoxical human warmth. In his private, and darker side, Scott returns to Lampman's world.

Lampman's dream is neither wholly of the past nor wholly of the future, neither wholly individual nor wholly collective, neither wholly spiritual nor wholly physical. It emerges implicitly from a kind of dialectic between "Reality" and "Solitude," "The Woodcutter's Hut" and "The City of the End of Things," from the double vision where he stands between past and future, autumn and spring.

As a token of the degree to which Lampman's vision has proved archetypically Canadian, let me suggest the contemplation of three poems. (Except for the season, one might add Roberts' "Tantramar Revisited.")

Bearing in mind the poles of Lampman's work as a whole, we begin with "In November," then turn to Birney's "November Walk Near False Creek Mouth," and finally to Dennis Lee's "Civil Elegies."

All three are descriptive and meditative poems, elegiac in tone. All three are set, initially or finally, in the fall. In all three the speaker is an *eiron*, looking forward and backward, aware of a past community, measuring his present isolation from it, preoccupied with the elusive, problematical possibility of recovering it.

The poems by Birney and Lee provide progressively fuller orchestrations of the elements we find in Lampman's work as a whole. Lee's "Civil Elegies" may well be the most comprehensive and intense articulation of the Canadian imagination as it has ramified and gathered density since Lampman's day — without, however, modifying its essential structure. We still move between the unreal city, with its noise and nervous activity, its cluttered space and polluted skies, and the reality of the land, its rocks, lakes, bush and apparent emptiness and silence. But the texture is more dense. We move between the old pioneer communities and the new branch-plant economy; between an older "national policy" and a more recent "policy of sellout;" between an older spiritual vision of evangelical Protestant or Jansenist Catholic and a newer material vision of entrepreneur and technocrat; between the fiasco of the 1837 rebellion and the fiasco of Viet Nam. We have added the Family Compact and William Lyon Mackenzie, Paul Martin and George Grant, Saint-Denys Garneau and Tom Thompson. But the poles of the vision and its general colouring remain the same. And it is perhaps an appropriate irony that the "Archer" which provides the link between Nathan Philips Square, a civic space, and primordial space, the city and the wilderness, past and present, is the work of the British sculptor, Henry Moore. But that is a minor point. The main point is that the City, its civic life, must be more thoroughly informed by that sense of primordial space if it is not to be empty — for both the dead and the living who congregate there, anxious and frustrated in their expectation of some profound community.

Lampman speaks of a "spectral happiness," Birney of the "unreached, unreachable nothing," Lee of a problematical "void." Each, though Birney might object, is an ironic affirmation of depth, a reality that underwrites or "understands" all life and community. And what speaks of this is not the voices of the City so much as Lampman's "voices of the earth," "the voices of earth's secret soul, / Uttering the mystery from which she came."

None of these writers makes his final appeal to a religious dogma, a philosophical doctrine, a scientific theory or a political program, but to the natural world. Whatever assurance or identity the speakers may have, it is to be found, ultimately, in their shared but individual relation to the earth. Lee concludes:

> Eearth, you nearest, allow me.
> Green of the earth and civil grey:
> within me, without me and moment by
> moment allow me for to
> be here is enough and earth you
> strangest, you nearest, be home.

I don't think Lampman would find himself disoriented in Lee's world. He might have to revise his vocabulary; he might have to admit a more ambiguous syntax; but he would not have to radically alter the structure of his vision.

ROBIN MATHEWS

LAMPMAN'S ACHIEVEMENT

Archibald Lampman's achievements are both intended and accidental, achievements one might say of conscious art and of historical
development. As a poet Lampman was a sensitive and meticulous
craftsman. His conscious achievement in the craft of poetry is
recognized increasingly as time passes. But the recognition he has
received as a result of the historical development of the tradition has
been a more bumpy and uncertain matter. Norman Shrive suggested a
good deal in that latter regard in an earlier discussion when he said that
the times of great concern about Lampman have been times, to use
Professor Shrive's unfortunate word, of "nationalism" in the country.

What Professor Shrive was saying, I take it, is that when the Canadian people turn seriously and with a measure of self-respect to their
own achievements as a people, they find in the work of Archibald
Lampman expression, art, poetry of astonishing beauty, relevance and
intelligence. When they turn away from a measured and reasonable
consideration of their own expression and art in order to lust — cyclo-
pean and tunnel visioned, envious and colonially self-denigrating —
after the sordid cultural flesh-pots of foreign, imperial nations, they find
in Lampman a pale and ineffectual aesthete, too trivial for serious attention. To coin an epigram, one might say that while licking the shoes of a
demanding master, the slave is not in a position to look his own brother
squarely in the eye.

One of the achievements of Lampman is to be good enough to
have survived the colonialist ignorance and the critical ineptitude of the
readership in his own country.

In speaking very briefly of Lampman's achievement, I assert that he achieved superbly as a poet. He is a major spokesman in the Canadian tradition. Only when we get Lampman into place *in our culture* will we be able to deal seriously *as Canadians* with poets like little Johnny Keats and Percy Shelley, for instance, and with the pee-wit pipers and pipsqueak propagandists for empire like William Carlos Williams, Charles Olson, and the whole Black Market *bunch* of poets. They cannot be termed a *school* of poets since sharks, I am told, do not travel in schools.

Lampman achieved superbly as a poet because he *intended* to do his best and because he was a significant artistic talent. But he achieved superbly, also, because he is woven into the fabric of the most relevant intellectual history of his time. He is of commanding importance to us, when we fully understand ourselves, because he took from the world what he needed in his thought — from the Greeks, from the English, from the writers of the U.S. — in a way which permitted him to address the major questions of the day, as he saw them, with a consciousness that was of his time, that was informed and relevant. But what is infinitely more important to the measure of his achievement is that he *lived* in the ideas of his own time *in this place*, structuring his thought from objects and experiences which are the furniture of our own lives.

Lampman used, moreover, the social furniture of his own place. He did not imitate ideas from the foreign world when he was doing his good work; he lived the ideas of the time in *his* place, with the furniture and the consciousness of that place. For that reason the foreign names plastered on Lampman's thought and expression are odious and inept, misleading and imprecise. If we are serious scholars, then we must strive for a precision of language to describe the writers in our tradition — a language that is able to contain their variety and catch their uniqueness. Lampman was not a Romantic poet; he was not a transcendentalist poet. Until we name our own creatures in our own garden, we will be Adams and Eves at a zoo, gaping at imported animals, trying to make a yankee cow and British goat define the peculiarities of the Canadian Buffalo.

Lampman *had* a Canadian milieu. For instance — only this — Lampman cared about "the stoic's grander portion — Dignity." He cared profoundly about the urge to virtue. He shared that concern with his contemporaries in Canada: Roberts, Lighthall, Goldwin Smith, Duncan Campbell Scott, and others. They worried the question of altruism with all its implications, and they worried it on home ground with a consciousness about it related to the furniture of their own lives and the state of their country in the world. That profound philosophical concern reverberates even yet in the imaginations of Canadians. In the section deling with "Philosophical Literature to 1910" in the *Literary History of Canada*, the authors, John A. Irving and A. H. Johnson, write about John Watson, a major internationally respected philospher at Queen's University from about 1873 to 1924, that he "was constantly on the war-path against Tyndall, Neitzsche, Spencer, and the American pragmatists; but he was also constantly building up constructive approaches to Kant, Hegel, and his contemporaries in the idealistic movement."[1] Watson was a contemporary of Lampman's, doing major work during Lampman's life. Much of his work was rejection — to put the matter in fairly crude terms — of self-regarding individualism and an attempt to discover a dialectical mode of credible human responsibility.

Lampman was one of those poets in our tradition who achieved a genuine habitation of this place. In doing so, he wrote in a way which informs, assists, lifts, criticizes, and cajoles any serious Canadian poet. Words are used well when they say things. Lampman says things in a language which, for us, moves towards full possibility of meaning because he achieved a genuine habitation of this place and could employ the experience of this place with precision.

If Lampman cannot be undestood by the British or the U.S. readers, the failure to understand is a function of imperial parochialism passing under the misnomer of cosmopolitanism. Their failure to understand is not a function of artistic incompetence on the part of Archibald Lampman.

"We cannot be patriotic as the Englishman is patriotic,"[2] Lampman writes. "The average American only loves and clings to his country as long as he can make money out of it,"[3] he goes on, in 1892, seeing distinctive differences among the Atlantic triangle English speaking peoples. Surely his achievement of a differing sense of reality should help us to form and clarify our way of seeing, not because we want to be patriotic Canadians, but because we want to be precise scholars and critics and poets who hone words about reality as we live it here until words let us think at the very sharp, invisible, pinpoint of truth.

NOTES

[1] John A. IRVING, adapted by A. H. JOHNSON, "Philosophical Literature to 1900," *Literary History of Canada*, ed. Carl F. KLINCK, Toronto, University of Toronto Press, 1965, p. 439.

[2] Archibald LAMPMAN, "At the Mermaid Inn", October 22, 1892, in Barrie DAVIES, ed., *Archibald Lampman: Selected Prose* (Ottawa: Tecumseh Press, 1975), p. 68.

[3] *Ibid.*

JAMES STEELE

LAMPMAN'S ACHIEVEMENT

I especially welcome the opportunity to participate on this panel, for I found myself yesterday disagreeing radically with Professor Dudek's paper, the central thesis of which — if it were to be accepted — would have a strong bearing on any assessment of Lampman's achievement. Professor Dudek, you will recall, argued that Lampman, in his very best poetry, employed that worn-out, "hypertrophied" verse-form known as the sonnet in order to express intellectually moribund, romantic thoughts. He concluded that Lampman's "ideas and his [verse] structures" formed "a kind of bulwark [in Lampman] against the flooding in of the twentieth century" and all of its soul-jarring realities. The corollary of Professor Dudek's argument, which also turns up as an editorial guideline in his critical anthology *The Making of Modern Poetry in Canada*, was this: those successors of Lampman who have employed the newer forms of free verse, imagism and expressionism — the poets of the modernist school to which Professor Dudek himself happens to belong — are more truly in touch with reality than was Lampman.

It seems to me, on the contrary, that almost everything of real substance that has been said by modernist poets in Canada was said first, in one way or another, by Lampman. (And by "real substance" I am not referring to the increased emphasis on subjectivity which modernists achieve through their rhetorical techniques and their particular modes of expression, but to their understanding of that subjectivity in the context of their world vision.) Lampman, it could be said, was the first poet of Canada's bourgeois intelligentsia[1] to sing of his disaffection for a social system which he nevertheless laboured to maintain. Poets before Lampman had, it is true, declared their dissatisfaction with the quality

125

of man's spiritual life in Canada, but they did not question the conventional religious and social values of their society. Alexander McLachlan, for example, insisted that every Jack was as good as his master and longed for the brotherhood of man. Nevertheless, he remained a staunch Gladstonian liberal with a strong affection for "acres of his own." Charles Sangster transcended the woes of material existence through a romanticism which was consistent with the creed of the Church of England, and he did so even while celebrating the beauty of free trade, industrialization and a harmonious relationship between master and servant. Lampman's proto-modernist feeling of alienation was much more thorough-going and profound than that of his predecessors. A moralistic rationale for it is suggested by his account of the perceptions of young Richard in "The Story of An Affinity"

> He saw how fair and beautiful a thing
> The movement of the busy world might be,
> Were men but just and gentle, but how hard,
> How full of doubt and pitiless life is,
> Seeing that ceaseless warfare is man's rule
> And all his laws and customs but thin lies
> To veil the pride and hatred of his heart.
> And utterances of spiritual beauty passed
> Between the babbling lips of men whose souls
> Remained as blind and impotent as before.
> He sat in the great churches and amid
> The grandeur of their silken ceremonies
> Heard the vaults thunder with the solemn chants
> And sacred hymns immeasurably sad,
> Wherein the universal human heart
> Had voiced the quietude of its vast despair,
> And all the awful weariness of life.
> He heard the pastor with impassioned tongue
> Preach the great love and brotherhood of man,
> While round him, silent in the velvet stalls,
> The rich and proud, the masters of this world,
> Sat moveless as the ever-living gods,
> While all that wordy thunder rolled and rang
> About their heads and pitiless ears in vain.
> He saw rude multitudes in wild despair
> Wear out their days in labour for small gain
> And sink care-weary into unknown graves,
> And how the strong, by chance and sleight made
>   great,
> Fattened and throve upon the general need,
> Hiding their cruel and remorseless hands
> Behind a mist of custom and the law,
> Huge offspring of a boundless anarchy!
> He saw the public leaders in whose charge
> Was given the chiefship and the common weal,
> Gulling men openly with fulsome lies;
> And on the trustful ignorance of the just
> And the blind greed and hatred of the base
> Building the edifice of their own power.

√This feeling of alienation also underlies the vision of estrangement in Lampman's poem "The Railway Station", the Checkhovian world-

126

weariness of soul in "In October" and the expressions of contempt in "To a Modern Politician" and "To a Millionaire" — all commonplace themes in later-day modernist Canadian poetry. Although Lampman apparently believed in the evolution of a world-soul from primitive beginnings to ever grander ends, he had despairingly modernist doubts about historical progress over the short run, doubts which he articulated, for example, in his sonnet "To Chaucer":

'Twas high mid-spring, when thou wert here on
   earth,
Chaucer, and the new world was just begun;
For thee 'twas pastime and immortal mirth
To work and dream beneath the pleasant sun,
Full glorious were the hearty ways of man,
And God above was great and wise and good,
Thy soul sufficient for its earthly span,
Thy body brave and full of dancing blood.
Such was thy faith, O master! We believe
Neither in God, humanity, nor self;
Even the votaries of place and pelf
Pass by firm-footed, while we build and weave
With doubt and restless care. Too well we see
The drop of life lost in eternity.

His modernist anxiety about the social implications of industrialization is to be found in "The City of the End of Things," and his pre-A.J.M. Smith scepticism about heroic individualism is, I suggest, the moral of "The King's Sabbath." It is also worth noting that this "poet of the confederation" was able to define his national identity only through the limited scope of landscape poetry. He avoided patriotic peotry, and in his critical statements, he informed his readers that patriotism for him was a matter of duty and honour rather than authentic impulse. Thus, even on the national question, Lampman's attitude was modernistically cosmopolitan (rather than internationalist) and equally rootless. Lampman anticipated later generations of poets in another important respect as well. When it came to overcoming his feelings of alienation, he sought poetic transcendence by writing about aesthetic pleasure and love, or about nature and his utopian dreams. What modernist poet, one might ask, has moved beyond this personalist idealism? Even in his literary criticism, Lampman, in his preoccupation with craft, was the first of the moderns.

Lampman's achievement is all the more remarkable when seen in the context of the social and ideological forces which were dominant in late Victorian Canada. By the 1870's, Canada's capitalist entrepreneurs had financed an industrial revolution and were firmly in control of the country's political parties and of the state patronage to which Lampman owed his relatively soft living.[2] Their categories of understanding were based in part on various kinds of idealism, both subjective and objective. This idealism also included a belief in historical progress, with a faith in individual heroism as a *sine qua non* of that progress. Lampman, whose intellect had been formed by a clerical father, private school and

Trinity College, and whose life's work was in the banking division of the Post Office, shared these notions. Yet even within the confines of this late-Victorian bourgeois idealism, he managed, as I have suggested, to anticipate much of the substance of the later modernist movement.

This achievement can be fully appreciated only by comparing it to that of some of his contemporaries, who perceived Canada's pre-monopoly, pre-imperialist age of industrial capitalism in very different terms. Unlike Charles G.D. Roberts, Lampman did not place his poetry at the service of those businessmen who were struggling for industrial expansion and world conquest in collaboration with the Anglo-Saxon races. Lampman, on the contrary, sang of his personal disaffection with such schemes. Unlike James B. DeMille, he did not use his pen to ridicule socialism and to vindicate the spirit of self-interest. Rather, Lampman offered his readers utopian dreams of a better world in which private enterprise did not flourish. And unlike William D. Lighthall, he did not react to his guilded age by recommending a return to the land and to small scale enterprise. Lampman accepted as inevitable the world of industrial capitalism while expressing — with all the humanist irony that he could muster — his distaste for the exploitation, alienation and tyranny which this system engendered. These were notable achievements for a poet of the 80's and 90's expressing himself with consummate skill in ancient verse forms, achievements which Lampman's modernist detractors, who lack his depth and breadth of vision, might learn from even today.

NOTES

[1] The word "intelligentsia" is used here in its technical Marxist sense to refer to a privileged intermediate stratum of society. Objectively, this stratum is a part of the working class inasmuch as it has only its mental power to sell for wages. Subjectively, however, a large part of it must be regarded as an adjunct of the ruling class inasmuch as it provides technical, and / or scientific, and / or ideological support for that class (or the state) in return for wages which are exceptionally high. In Lampman's day, this stratum would have included, among other, most teachers, clergymen and senior civil servants.

[2] Lampan's position in the Post Office was secured for him by Sir Archibald Campbell (who on another occasion gave Sir Hugh Allan the lucrative postal subsidies which formed a large part of the Allan fortune), and his civil service wage apparently rose over the years from $9.00 to $16.00 per week for a 6-hour day. Some idea of contemporary wage rates for other occupations in the city of Ottawa may be obtained from a perusal of the *Royal Commission on the Relations of Labour and Capital, 1899*: child labourers in a saw-mill and a box-factory were paid $1.50 a week, and the going rate for child labour in a match factory was $2.30. Log-makers were paid $5.00 (plus board) for a week of 12-hour days; mill-workers were paid $8.00 for a week of 12-hour days; and a foreman in a bakery earned $10.00 to $12.00. Thus Lampman's rate of pay was about three or four times that received by an adult industrial worker. Relative to his society, he was therefore probably better off at the end of his career than most academics attending this conference are with respect to theirs. (See Greg KEALEY, ed., *Canada Investigates Industrialism*, (Toronto, 1973), pp. 192-220, *passim*.)

PROGRAM OF
THE LAMPMAN SYMPOSIUM
1975

Friday, May 2: Registration and Reception

Saturday, May 3

Chairman: Glenn Clever

9:00 a.m. — Panel: Biographical Discussion
            Chairman: Fred Cogswell
            Panelists: Barrie Davies
                       Ralph Gustafson
                       Margaret Whitridge

10:30 a.m. — Paper: "Archibald Lampman and His Critics,"
             Michael Gnarowski

11:30 a.m. — Paper: "The Frogs: An Exercise in Reading Lampman,"
             Carl F. Klinck

Chairman: Lorraine McMullen

2:00 p.m. — Paper: "Lampman and the Death of the Sonnet," Louis
            Dudek

3:00 p.m. — Paper: "Sweet Patience, adn Her Guest, Reality: the Son-
            nets of Archibald Lampman," Louis K.
            MacKendrick

129

4:00 p.m. — Paper: " 'So Deathly Silent': the Resolution of Pain and Fear in the Poetry of Lampman and D.C. Scott," Dick Harrison

8:30 p.m. — Reading of Lampman poems by poets attending the Symposium

Sunday, May 4

Chairman: Agnes Nyland, S.S.A.

10:00 a.m. — Paper: "The Forms of Nature: Some of the Philosophical and Aesthetic Bases of Lampman's Nature Poetry," Barrie Davies

11:00 a.m. — Paper: "Lampman — the Theory and Practice of Craft," John Nause

Chairman: Frank M. Tierney

2:00 p.m. — Paper: "The New Lampman", Bruce Nesbitt

3:00 p.m. — Panel: Lampman's Achievement
Chairman: Carl F. Klinck
Panelists: Fred Cogswell
Sandra Djwa
D.G. Jones
Robin Mathews
James Steele

Grateful acknowledgement is made to the Canada Council for financial assistance and to the Public Archives of Canada for assistance in arranging the display of Lampman memorabilia.

MARGARET COULBY WHITRIDGE

THE LAMPMAN MANUSCRIPTS
— A Brief Guide

Four Canadian institutions currently retain the large majority of Lampman Papers known to exist — the manuscripts and correspondence of Archibald Lampman. All are available to research scholars. These are the University of Toronto, including the main library and the library of Trinity College, the Public Archives of Canada and the Parliamentary Library in Ottawa, and Simon Fraser University Library in British Columbia. Smaller collections can be consulted at Queen's University, the Women's Canadian Historical Society, McGill University, Ottawa Public Library and the University of New Brunswick's Rufus Hathaway Collection. Letters to Lampman are also retained by the Toronto Public Library and letters about Lampman may be found in various collections in the Public Archives, the Ontario Archives, possibly at Cornell University, and in a surprising number of private hands, including those of Lampman's relatives and the descendants of friends, chiefly in Ontario.

Not all of Lampman's letters and manuscripts known to have existed have yet been found.

The most important collection is, rightfully, retained in the Public Archives of Canada in Ottawa and it would seem to be highly desirable for the Archives to have, on microfilm or in photocopy, copies of all the other documents. It would then become a true research centre in the city where Lampman lived, wrote and died, for Lampman scholars. This small band has grown from about half a dozen in 1968 to probably one hundred and fifty today, all bent on exploring and laying bare that important corner of Canada's literary history — the Confederation Group of Writers from 1880 to 1900.

A brief guide to the currently known collections has been drawn up and is appended here for the information of all those interested in Lampman materials:

1. *Library of Parliament, Ottawa*
   Four bound manuscript volumes of poems:
   (a) *Miscellaneous Poems* (ca 1883-1888) 190 pages
       Catalogue No. PS8473 / A56 / A6
   (b) *Alcyone* (ca 1898) 120 pages
       Catalogue No. PS8473 / A72
   (c) *David and Abigail* (ca 1887) 124 pages
       Catalogue No. PS8473 / A56 / D3
   (d) *The Story of an Affinity* (April 1894) 74 pages
       Catalogue No. PS8473 / A56 / A58

2. *McGill University, Montreal*
   Letters — Fifteen holograph letters from Archibald Lampman to William D. Lighthall, Montreal dated September 14, 1888 to November 7, 1898.
   Poems — Two manuscript poems, "Winter" and "Ballad of Summer's Rest, undated, 5 pages.
   Portrait— Signed head and shoulders portrait by A. D. Patterson, inscribed "Archibald Lampman 1861-1899".

3. *Ottawa Public Library*
   Letter — One page memorandum from Archibald Lampman to W. A. Code, no date, circa 1896.

4. *Public Archives of Canada, Ottawa*
   Five volumes of *Lampman Papers*, Catalogue No. MG29 / D59
   Letters — One hundred and twelve letters from Archibald Lampman to E. W. Thomson dated March 28, 1890 to November 22, 1898.
   — One letter from Archibald Lampman to D.C. Scott dated July 29, 1898.
   — Twenty-six letters from E. W. Thomson to Archibald Lampman dated July 1891 to October 4, 1897.
   — Two letters from D. C. Scott to Archibald Lampman dated April 28 and May, 1897.

   Poems — Twenty-two rough manuscript work-books containing over four hundred draft poems dating from 1883 to 1899.
   — One final bound manuscript volume of poems written 1894-99, 104 pages.
   — Holograph poems, signed and occasionally dated.
   — Christmas cards printed privately and distributed jointly by D. C. Scott and Archibald Lampman, 1890, 1894 (See also Trinity College, Toronto and University of New Brunswick holdings).

Prose — Novel, unfinished, 64 pages, no date (1884)
— Two fairy tales, "The Fairy Fountain", 1885, 31 pages and "Hans Fingerhut's Frog Lesson", 1885, 23 pages.
— Six prose notes about trips etcetera.
— Two social essays, "Happiness: A Preachment", July 1896, 24 pages and an untitled essay on Socialism, no date (ca 1895), 13 pages.
— Nine critical essays:
   "Armadis of Gaul", 1884, 7 pages.
   "George F. Cameron", no date, 4 pages.
   "Keats", 1893, 39 pages.
   "The Modern School of Poetry in England", February, 1885, 14 pages.
   "Poetic Interpretation", no date, 38 pages.
   "The Poets", no date, 45 pages
   "The Poetry of Byron", no date, 23 pages
   "Style", no date, 37 pages
   "Two Canadian Poets: A Lecture", 1891, 67 pages

The Lampman Papers also include manuscript poems by the poet's father, the Rev. Archibald Lampman, who sometimes wrote under the pen-name "Crowquill". They include a seventy-page manuscript by Duncan Campbell Scott on Henrich Heine, a signed manuscript poem by Scott, "After the Battle" and poems initialled and written by Bliss Carman ("On an Old Ball Programme") and Charles G. D. Roberts, ("Remember One Day In Quebec").

Lampman's correspondence and his manuscripts have been inventoried and paged. A Finding Guide is available to scholars at the Public Archives.

5. *Queen's University, Kingston*
   Letters — Six letters from Archibald Lampman to Horace Scudder, Boston, dated 1892-1895.
   — Six Letters written to Copeland and Day, Boston publisher in 1895 and 1896.
   — Copies of thirteen letters written by Archibald Lampman to Bliss Carman from 1889-1892.

   Composite Manuscript, 39 leaves. Part of the printer's copy of *Lyrics of Earth* published by Copeland and Day, Boston, 1895. Thirty pages contain holograph poems while nine pages contain printed poems, cut from periodicals, three of them corrected by Lampman.

6. *Simon Fraser University, British Columbia*
   Three manuscript volumes, one hundred and fifty-seven letters, miscellaneous poems, Lampman's sketchbook, photographs and other memorabilia.

Prose — "The Character and Poetry of Keats", holograph, 132 pages.

Poems — Untitled volume of poems, holograph, 149 pages.
— *Alcyone*, inscribed with explanatory note regarding publication by Duncan Campbell Scott. James Ogilvy, Ottawa, 1899, 110 pages
— Miscellanous holograph poems, including ten poems written by Lampman for Maud Playter, poems written to his sister, Isabelle Voorhis, and drafts of poems held by Lampman's mother. 42 leaves.
— Fragment of poem beginning "not like thy brother death with massive tread..." (Love and Death).

Letters — Letters from Lampman to his wife, Maud Playter Lampman, from July 15, 1885 to October 4, 1895. 103 letters.
— Letters from Lampman to his mother, his sister Isabelle and his daughter Nathalie. 5 letters.
— Letters to Archibald Lampman from friends and writers including Bliss Carman, Charles G. D. Roberts, Joseph Edmund Collins, Gilbert Parker, William Wilfred Campbell, Isabelle and Ernest Voorhis, Annie Lampman Jenkins, Professor M. C. Tyler, Eben Picken, Edmund C. Hedman, W. D. Howitts, J. E. Wetherell, F. G. Scott, J. O. Miller and Gilbert Aberdeen. 20 letters.
— Correspondence between members of Lampman's family and friends. 6 letters.

Memorabilia
— Lampman's sketchbook, family photographs, certificates etcetera.

7. *Toronto Public Library*
    The *Melvin Hammond Papers* contain the texts of two letters written by Charles G. D. Roberts to Archibald Lampman dated December 18, 1888 and September 23, 1882 (partial).

8. *Trinity College, University of Toronto*
    The Library of Trinity College contains the Minutes of Trinity Literary Institute, 1879-1882 of which Lampman was an active member. Some of the minutes are written in his meticulous penmanship during his term as secretary. The Library also retains the files of the university periodical, *Rouge et Noir* from 1880 to 1886 and its successor, the *Trinity University Review* which published much of Lampman's early poetry and prose.

Letters — Christmas cards and letters sent to the Rev. Charles H. Shortt from 1890 to 1898, (1890, 1893, 1894, 1895, 1896, 1898).
— Microfilm copies of letters written by Archibald Lampman to

Mrs. May McKeggie from September 24, 1884 to January 10, 1896. 12 letters. Originals belong to Miss C. Blackstock.
— Microfilm copies of letters written by Miss Annie Lampman to Mrs. May McKeggie from December 30, 1884 to April 26, 1891. 5 letters. Originals belong to Miss C. Blackstock, Toronto.

9. *University of New Brunswick Library, Fredericton*
The *Rufus Hathaway Collection* contains two signed holograph poems by Archibald Lampman and several related letters.

Poems — Signed manuscripts of two sonnets by Lampman, "By the Sea" and "To the Warbling Vireo", no date, 1 page each.

Letters — Letter form Bliss Carman to Duncan C. Scott, December 1889, discussing Lampman's and Scott's work.
— Two letters from Duncan C. Scott to Edwin Doak Mead, editor of the *New England Magazine* dated February 2 and March 7, 1899 about Lampman's work.
— Letter from Rufus Hathaway to Archibald Lampman, son of the poet in Toronto enquiring about his father's work, dated February 23, 1933.

10. *University of Toronto Library*
A bound manuscript volume of ninety-two poems, Catalogue No. 434453, forms the major portion of this collection, together with several manuscript poems and eight letters.

Poems — "The Child's Music Lesson", partial manuscript by Lampman, 2 pages, no date.
— "October" initialled manuscript poem by Lampman dated October 1884, 2 pages.
— Signed manuscript volume of poems inscribed "Christmas 1889", Catalogue No. 434453, 163 pages.

Letters — Three letters written by Duncan C. Scott to Lampman dated August 2, 1898; August 30, 1898; September 16, 1898.
— Two letters written by Lampman to Duncan C. Scott on February 16, 1898 and September 10, 1898.
— Three letters written by Lampman to J. E. Wetherell, Strathroy, Ontario on November 14, 1892; December 7, 1892; April 1, 1893.

11. *Women's Canadian Historical Society, Toronto*
Poem — "The Passing of Spring", signed manuscript poem by Lampman, no date, 1 page.

In addition to these primary sources of Lampman materials, related letters and documents referring to Lampman will be found in the following papers in the *Public Archives of Canada*, Ottawa:

Dr. E. K. Brown, Catalogue No. MG30 / D83.

Mrs. H. O. McCurry (nee Dorothy Lampman Jenkins), Catalogue No. MG30 / D!98.

Duncan Campbell Scott, Catalogue No. MG30 / D118

Sir John Thompson, Catalogue No. MG26 / D and the *Thompson Letterbooks*, Volume 253, pages 229-230.

Ernest Voorhis (Lampman's brother-in-law), Catalogue No. MG30 / D212.

The *Ontario Archives* in Toronto also contain related correspondence in the papers of *Sir Alexander Campbell*, Postmaster General of Canada: Four letters from Archibald Campbell, Toronto to his father requesting employment in the Civil Service for Lampman dated November 25 and November 29, 1882; February 22, 1883 and February 12, 1884.

CONTRIBUTORS

BARRIE DAVIES is Associate Professor of English at University of New Brunswick. He has published a number of articles on Archibald Lampman and is the editor of *Archibald Lampman: Selected Prose*.

SANDRA DJWA is Associate Professor of English at Simon Fraser University. She has published widely in the field of Canadian literature and in 1974 published *E. J. Pratt: The Evolutionary Vision*. Professor Djwa has a selected edition of the poetry of Charles Heavysege in press with the University of Toronto, and has been working for several years on a study of "English Canadian Poetry, 1628-1970."

LOUIS DUDEK is Professor of English at McGill University. He is well known as poet, critic, and editor and has been active in little magazines and small presses since the 1940's. He is co-editor of *The Making of Modern Poetry in Canada*.

MICHALE GNAROWSKI is Professor of English at Carleton University. He is general editor of the Carleton Library Series and of the McGraw-Hill Ryerson series Critical Views on Canadian Writers, co-editor of *The Making of Modern Poetry in Canada* and compiler of *A Concise Bibliography of English Canadian Literature*.

RALPH GUSTAFSON is Professor of English at Bishop's University. A well known poet, his most recent poetry collection, *Fire on Stone*, won the Governor General's Award for Poetry, 1974. His articles and essays have appeared in a number of journals. He is editor of the Penguin anthologies of Canadian poetry.

DICK HARRISON teaches at University of Alberta. He has published articles and reviews on prairie fiction and contributed a chapter to *Men in Scarlet*, McClelland and Stewart, 1974.

DOUGLAS G. JONES is Professor of English at Université de Sherbrooke, He is a poet, a founder and member of the editorial board of *Ellipse*, and author of *Butterfly on Rock: A Study of Themes and Images in Canadian Literature*.

CARL F. KLINCK is Professor of English at University of Western Ontario. His scholarly achievements in Canadian literature are well known. Professor Klinck is general editor of *The Literary History of Canada* and co-editor with R. E. Watters of *Canadian Anthology*. He has edited and introduced a number of works by early Canadian writers and published many articles and reviews.

LOUIS K. MACKENDRICK is Assistant Professor of English at the University of Windsor. He has published articles and reviews on a number of writers and wrote the Introduction to Robert Barr's *The Measure of the Rule* in University of Toronto Canadian Literature in Reprint series.

ROBIN MATHEWS is Associate Professor at Carleton University where he teaches Canadian literature. He has written articles on Canadian intellectual history and on nineteenth-century writers.

JAMES STEELE is Chairman of the Department of English at Carleton University. He has written articles on Canadian politics, the national question and Thomas Gray, and was a co-editor of *The Struggle for Canadian Universities*.

BRUCE NESBITT is Associate Professor at Simon Fraser University. He is Editor of the annual World Shakespeare Bibliography and of the annual bibliography of Canadian literature published in the *Journal of Canadian Fiction*, and edited *Earle Birney* in the McGraw-Hill Ryerson series Critical Views of Canadian Writers. Professor Nesbitt is working on a definitive edition of the poetry of Archibald Lampman.

MARGARET WHITRIDGE is Chief of an Information Division in Health and Welfare Canada. She contributed the Introduction to University of Toronto Reprint of *Poems of Archibald Lampman* and published *Lampman's Kate*, a collection of the previously unpublished love poems of Lampman to Katherine Waddell. *Lampman's Sonnets*, a collection with an introduction is in press and Dr. Whitridge expects to complete her biographical study of Lampman shortly.

a Bi
ve

etwork